DESPAIR AND HOPE
My journey to freedom

Tytus Sas Komarnicki

Translated from the French by
Juliusz Komarnicki

Photos by Hanna Komarnicki

Despair and Hope

Published by The Conrad Press in the United Kingdom 2022

Tel: +44(0)1227 472 874
www.theconradpress.com
info@theconradpress.com

ISBN 978-1-914913-87-7

Copyright © Tytus Sas Komarnicki, 2022

The moral right of Tytus Sas Komarnicki to be identified as author of this work has been asserted in accordance with the Copyright, Designs and Patents Act 1988.

All rights reserved.

Typesetting and Cover Design by: Charlotte Mouncey, www.bookstyle.co.uk
The Conrad Press logo was designed by Maria Priestley.

Printed and bound in Great Britain by Clays Ltd, Elcograf S.p.A.

Author's dedication in his diary
À ma femme bien aimée
Souvenirs de nos mois de séparation.
Toutes mes pensées appartenaient
à toi, chérie, et à mes gosses
dans ce temps de lutte!
Tito
28.9.1943 - 7.12.1943

This book is dedicated to the loving memory of my parents Tytus and Chiara Sas Komarnicki.

Also, a very special thanks to my daughters, Caterina Selz and Julia Seebacher, for their financial aid without which this book would not have been possible.

I would also like to thank my dear wife Hanna for producing such lovely photographs during our two trips to illustrate my father's diary of his journey.

Juliusz Komarnicki - May 2022

Translator's foreword to *Despair and Hope*

by Juliusz Komarnicki

Many years ago, when my dear mother was already fairly old, she entrusted me with a black notebook explaining that this was the diary that my father wrote, when he had to undertake an epic journey in order to escape Gestapo agents in wartime France in 1943.

For many years I left this diary to one side thinking that I would try and read it one day as my father's writing was most difficult to decipher. Finally, once I was retired, I got round to reading it, and soon found that I was unable to put it down. Having worked in the publishing world all my life, I immediately thought that perhaps we could make a book out of it, and I got down to translating the diary into English so as to reach a wider audience.

My photographer wife Hanna then suggested that we follow my father's footsteps and take photos of all the places mentioned in his diary. During the following two autumns of 2017 and 2018 we embarked on our own experience – first in France, Andorra and Spain, and then in Madrid and Portugal, and finally in Gibraltar.

The photographic results were most satisfactory and above all our journey was a very emotional experience for me personally. To re-live a journey that my father had undertaken, under very arduous and harrowing conditions, seventy-five years previously, turned out to be something very special.

The reader might be somewhat confused by all the Polish names in the text, especially in the first chapter. I can say that I don't know personally who they were, as I was only four years old at that time. But the owners of those names were undoubtedly collaborators and colleagues of my father, due to his crucial dual position in Grenoble; firstly, as the Polish delegate of the Polish Red Cross in France and secondly, as the envoy of the Polish government-in-exile to the Vichy government, being in a covert position of which the Germans took a dim view. His activities soon got noticed by the Gestapo. He had to go into hiding – first, in the famous Grande Chartreuse monastery and then, with a friendly family in the Château of Maubec, near Grenoble.

He then decided that he had to leave as soon as possible when things were hotting up. In September 1943, after the armistice with Italy, he was called by the Polish government-in-exile to come to London as quickly as possible to take up a more senior position. Hence, this escape journey.

Before the war my father had held several key positions in the Polish diplomatic service. For several years he had not only been the Polish delegate to the League of Nations which was the predecessor of the United Nations, as well as being a director of the International Labour Office, which were, and still are, both based in Geneva; from 1937 to 1940 he was the Polish ambassador to Switzerland, based in Bern. In May 1940, after the change of government in Poland, he was forced to leave his post and he was offered the position as director of the Polish Red Cross in France, first in Bordeaux, then in Marseilles and as from 1942, in Grenoble.

To aid readers' understanding, it might help to outline the role of some of the main characters in the text:

Bobrowski was a close friend of my father and his constant companion for the five weeks of their journey together.

Mierzynski was my father's chief assistant in Grenoble.

Waclav, pronounced 'Vacwav', or Wacio pronounced 'Vacio' was my father's brother and held the position of the minister of justice of the Polish government-in-exile in London.

- Chiara was my father's Italian-born wife living with my sister Terenia and me in Villard-de-Lans, a mountain village about 30 km away from Grenoble.
- Szumlakowski was the Polish government-in-exile's ambassador in Madrid and a former good friend of my father when living in Geneva in the 1930s.

Please see the Appendix for notes on other key references in the diary.

Juliusz Komarnicki - May 2022

Contents

Translator's foreword to *Despair and Hope*   5

by Juliusz Komarnicki   5

Chapter 1: Preparations for a journey - September 1943   9

Chapter 2: The journey in France   14

Chapter 3: Andorra   27

Chapter 4: Spain: Puigcerdá to Barcelona   40

Chapter 5: Barcelona   43

Chapter 6: The taxi journey to Madrid   55

Chapter 7: Waiting in Madrid   59

Chapter 8: The train journey through Spain and Portugal   75

Chapter 9: Gibraltar   80

Chapter 10: The flight to England and arrival   94

Chapter 11: The endless wait in London   98

Notes to accompany the text   107

Chapter 1

Preparations for a journey - September 1943

The idea of my journey has become more actual ever since the 8th of September 1943, which was the day that the Armistice was signed between Italy and the Allies. It was then that I last saw Mr Mierzynski in Grenoble at the Villa de la Tronche and I had my last conversation with Mr Kowalkowski, who is the head of 'Monika'.

At that moment, I concluded that the Polish Foreign Office has minimal interest in my activities in France. It has always been the same personal jealousies and the fear that my prestige might go up significantly with Mr Frankowski. In my opinion, the secret organisation Monika is involved in dangerous activities, also taking over other clandestine organisations, all under the quasi-dictatorial rule of Mr Kowalkowski.

Apart from that, for several months the necessary funds have not been forthcoming. I've found that I'm no longer able to organise and direct the Polish organisation's activities in France. Also, my brother Waclaw sends me telegrams through Mr Celinski in Switzerland insisting more and more that I should leave. As I thought, it was impossible that I could go if this did not correspond with the foreign minister's will. I believe they would be happy if I would just disappear from France. Ever since Morawski was appointed as the diplomatic representative in Angers, my situation with the Vichy government has become, without doubt, stranger than ever.

Wednesday the 22nd of September

I ask my secretary Mr Mierzynski to come to the Château of Maubec, near Voiron, where I'm staying. It is the first time that he comes and he does not know this address. Poor Mr Mierzynski; he arrives in the middle of a storm and the torrential rain means he gets soaked to the skin. Who could foresee that this would be the last time that we would see each other? I give him all the necessary instructions for my departure, planned for the first half of October. We get so absorbed in our conversation that I completely forget the coffee that I was preparing in an electric kettle. After nearly two hours, I remember and find the kettle damaged and the coffee dried up to a fine powder.

Thursday the 23rd of September

I'm already feeling better than previously now that I've finally made my decision to leave and I've given my orders so that everything goes into motion. I was most worried before deciding. I did not want to abandon my position until the end, nor leave my wife Chiara and the kids, and there was also the uncertainty of my future in London and the perils of the Pyrenees crossing. The only bright side is the reunion with my dear brother Wacio.

Friday the 24th of September

A disastrous day! As I came back from my morning walk, I'm met on the stairs by Mrs Dechandol who informs me that my '*Bouton de Rose*' (Mrs Simone's code name) is waiting for me in my room. I go in and she tells me in a solemn voice that yesterday, at 5 pm, the Mierzynski couple got arrested by the

Gestapo. Bobrowski, who was with them, with a quick presence of mind, managed to get away. What a disaster!

Nevertheless, Mrs Simone informs me that he had already arranged many details of my journey before being arrested. I give more instructions to Mrs Simone, and beg her to get in contact with Colonel Jakliez to fix the date of my departure.

I'm so upset by this news concerning the Mierzynski couple that my slight stomach indisposition becomes much worse, which is of some concern as I might not have the necessary strength to face the strains of my forthcoming journey.

Saturday the 25th of September

Today Mrs Simone came back to see me. A terrible storm meant she arrived soaked to the skin! She tells me that I have to leave on the 28th of September, which will most likely be the last departure for Spain this year. I have to be in Grenoble on Monday the 27th and she will arrange all my meetings, and especially the most important one with Colonel Jakliez. She will personally go this evening to Villard-de-Lans to warn Chiara.

I hardly eat anything all day. Good old Wolf comes to see me and sorts out everything for my French ID. It's funny this friendship with this Polish communist who used to be a fighter for the Reds in Spain. But he is a good chap, whose noble character, together with his naïve approach, is exploited by people in Moscow's pay. He rendered me many services which I have repaid and especially by looking after his son.

Sunday the 26th of September

My last Sunday in France. It's raining very hard again. I go to the local parish church which is nearer than the Dominican convent, where I always enjoyed hearing Mass. As usual, the parish priest's sermon is stupid. He quotes the German soldiers as examples of patriotism!

Mrs Dechandol makes me a rice soup which is the only food that I have all day. I feel physically ill and sometimes rather disheartened. But I pull myself together and I trust in God that all will go well.

In the afternoon I pack up all my belongings as I don't want to leave many things here so that Chiara does not have any transport problems. Most of my stuff I will take away by taxi tomorrow morning.

Monday the 27th of September

I take a taxi from Voiron to Grenoble and go to 11 rue de Bizanet which I had left on the 19th of March after my failed arrest by the Carabinieri. I arrive at about 10 am. A rather frightened Jankowski greets me on the stairs and helps me with my luggage. With the rest I go to Mrs Simone who lives in a little house nearby. She greets me most cordially and makes me a nice cup of tea.

I then see Sienkiewski through whom I can inform Kowalkowski and Danbrowski about my decisions. Next Ambassador Grzybowski arrives to whom I explain the reasons for my imminent departure with which he fully agrees.

Given the general situation I can't give him the full details. Next comes Colonel Jakiez, who gives me all the practical information regarding my departure. He very much hopes that I shall be able to talk to Sosukowski about his security and that of Colonel Fyola who was so persecuted by General Sikorski.

Afterwards I go up to the second floor to Miss Lubczynska's

room from which I can see when Chiara arrives. She arrives an hour and a half late, laden with so much luggage and with a rucksack and other parcels in her hands. She runs into my arms and we remain a long time clinging tightly to each other and sobbing. It is a very emotional moment for both of us.

We then prepare a delicious lunch. We have a long time for ourselves until 4 pm, but our conversation is uncoordinated given that we have so many things to talk about, and we speak as if in a fever.

Chiara leaves at 6 pm for Voiron and I take the train an hour later. But before leaving I receive Mrs Gout and Mr De Birou, Mr Siekierski, Mr Marczewski, and at the end, Mr Jakubowski and Mr Zielinski. They have just arrived in Grenoble and on their way decided to propose that I leave given my precarious position and the general situation. They don't see how I can, in any way, continue my activities. We take our leave of each other, not without much emotion after the months of our close and friendly collaboration.

I then leave rue de Bizanet for the last time. As I walk through the streets of Grenoble, I notice how many German soldiers are around. Just as it's getting dark at 8 pm, I get to Voiron and Chiara comes to greet me in the park, accompanied by Mrs Dechandol. We dine together in our flat and chat for a long time, taking advantage of every moment that remains before this cruel separation. For how long will we be apart?

Mrs Bobrowska comes for a moment together with Mr Wolf. She also finds herself in the same situation as Chiara. It's very late by the time we get to bed.

Chapter 2

The journey in France

Tuesday the 28th of September 1943 - The day of departure
We get up early and spend the morning in an atmosphere full of tenderness and melancholy. Mrs Simone comes to see me for the last time to get my final instructions, and to pay the bill. Then the three of us go to Pavot to buy some fruit. I have lunch with Chiara in our room.

In the afternoon, we go to the Dominican convent where I make my confession. It's mostly a grey and sombre day with the occasional rain shower. but better than in the previous days.

Chiara gets fits of depression and occasionally starts sobbing, and I try to do everything in my power to distract her from the main objects of our shared worries. However, we often have very moving and touching moments together. The Dechandols are very much intrigued by all the preparations for my departure. They don't know that my journey is definite, but I do have to face crucial decisions and dangers. I only tell their father where I'm going. He is a discreet person and will know how to keep a secret. He offers his services for other Poles who will still need his safe haven.

And finally, the moment of our separation has arrived. Our last supper, where our tears mingle with our food. My God, we shall not be together for Christmas Eve. It's moving to receive the envelope with *oplatek* and hair-clippings of my kids. Terenia has written such a beautiful letter and I have to re-read it with much emotion several times. After supper we each write letters to each other for the 4th of October, which is our wedding anniversary, and a few lines that we shall read after my departure.

With my rucksack on my back, I go downstairs and take my leave of the kind Dechandol family. They have been excessively kind to me, and they are such good people.

I leave at 9.15 pm and the night is already very dark and it's pouring with rain! I renounce my walking stick and instead choose an umbrella. My rucksack is full and Chiara has knotted another little sack on top, which contains my little cushion and mountaineering shoes. She walks with me to the park where we separate near a small fountain. We cover each other in kisses and embrace very tightly for a long moment. From the road, I can still see the dear silhouette of my adorable wife in the window of my room, and we keep on repeating, '*Au revoir, au revoir!*'

The night is very dark and I have difficulty finding the park's main gate. Luckily. Chiara insisted that I take a little electric torch and I don't know how I would have arrived in Moirans without it. It is still pouring, but I'm well-protected by this large umbrella which could accommodate all our family. In no time I arrive at the station of Moirans which is 5 kilometres away.

Goodbye good restaurants of Moirans! The Hôtel Beau Séjour, the Brasserie Lyonnaise are places where I enjoyed some great meals these last months, together with Mierzynski, Jakubowski, Celinski, Jakliez and others. It was my 'office' where we would settle many matters during the course of these luncheons.

Here is the little road which takes one from the main Grenoble-Moirans highway to the station of Moirans. How many times the poor Mierzynski waited for me here! He was a loyal, faithful, and dedicated colleague and his memory will accompany me on my journey. I'm leaving the places where I have spent a few months of my life in hiding.

Finally, I'm at the station, which is nearly deserted. The train for Grenoble arrives at 23.07. The train is full but, after a few minutes, I find a good seat in third class which I occupy even though I have a second-class ticket. Dressed in my windcheater, with a large rucksack and my knickerbockers, I don't look like an ordinary tourist!

After Avignon, where I had to change at 3 am, the train was also packed, and I had to stand for two hours which was very tiring. Travelling conditions in France are most horrendous at present, and as time passes, so I drift away from my dear ones. The dice has been thrown and may God protect me!

Wednesday the 29th of September

We arrive in Toulouse at about 10 am, an hour late. It's a grey and dull day. I just want to get to the hotel to have a wash and lie down a bit before lunch. The station's Hôtel Terminus is very near but I'm advised to try the Hôtel Regina just opposite.

It's the first time that I register in a hotel under Mr Charles Dumont's name as a French citizen, born in Paris in 1890 and domiciled in Chambéry, 27 Place Saint-Léger, transferred recently to Lyon and, as profession, an agricultural engineer. As I go up to my room, I notice that the hotel is full of Germans and French police. It's the HQ of the Gestapo! I feel somewhat uneasy in this circle, and I get the idea that they might want to check on my papers and possibly arrest me in such a stupid way even before I have started my journey. I therefore just get washed and, instead of lying down, I go downstairs and into the street for a few minutes. Then I come back to reception to say that I want to cancel the room as I've been invited by my friend, whom I just met outside by pure chance! Very decently, they only charge me fifteen francs for the use of the bathroom.

I leave my belongings at the station's left luggage store and then wander aimlessly around the streets of Toulouse. Unfortunately, my gallstones give me trouble and I even pass some blood which worries me somewhat given my long trek ahead. I have lunch at the Restaurant Conti, Place du Capitol, which is quite good and well-frequented.

At 5 pm I get on the train in the direction of Pau and then get off at the little station of Boussens. Here we take a bus to Salias de Salat. At the bus station I see Brodnicki and my travel companion Bobrowski. I notice that the three buses are full of Poles who undoubtedly share the same aim. It's a mass evacuation!

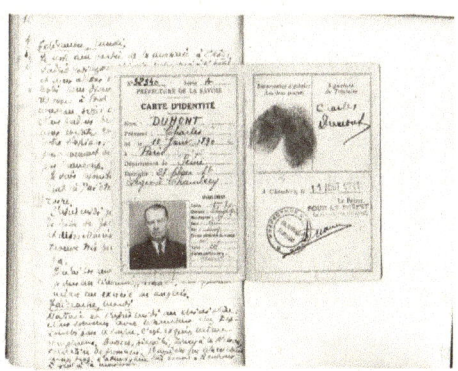

False ID

Day 1: Thursday the 30th of September

We get up at 5 am. The organisers bring us breakfast consisting of coffee, two hard-boiled eggs and some bread and butter. At 7.15 am Bobrowski, Barzykowski and I get into the bus that takes us back to Boussens and then back by train to Toulouse. In the end, this excursion to Salias de Salat was a complete waste of time! They could have easily given us all the necessary instructions in Toulouse. But these are military precautions which sometimes are somewhat infantile.

At the railway station Mr Leonard Rudowski, the local Polish delegate in Toulouse, and Mr Wodzicki, a technical counsellor at the Polish Office, whom I had appointed just a few months earlier, come to meet me. Yesterday, they had come to meet all the trains but missed me as I took the Hôtel Terminus exit. They then notified the Grenoble office that I had not been on the train. I sincerely hope that this false news never reached my Chiara as this would have really scared her. We all go together to Mr Rudowski's place where he very kindly provides us with a second breakfast, but this time it is somewhat beefed-up sausages, good lard and a glass of good wine and some tea.

We go to an excellent 'black' restaurant at midday, which boasts a fantastic menu and two sublime wines. Bobrowski pays the bill. We go back to Mr Rudowski's flat where we rest for an hour and a half. At 4 pm, he and his flat companion, Mr Kotodynski, serve us high tea.

It's at Toulouse railway station where I go with Bobrowski that Mr Barzykowski introduces us to our guide Louis who will take us through the 'forbidden zone'. He is known to be very brave and resourceful. But once we are sitting in the carriage, Louis comes close to our window with another fellow. We subsequently hear that Louis had just learnt that the Gestapo had come looking for him in his apartment, which means that he has to go into hiding for a few days and it will be his friend who will replace him as our guide.

Day 1 (continued): Thursday the 30th of September - Toulouse to Foix

Our train from Toulouse leaves at 18.45 in the direction of Ax-les-Thermes. We pass the town Sauverdun, where a road takes you to Mazères which is where I last met Stani in 1941. He had been our chauffeur at the Embassy in Switzerland before the war. He had been imprisoned in the Vernet d'Ariège's infamous German concentration camp.

At 9 pm, Bobrowski and I get off at the little station of Saint-Jean-de-Verges. It's very dark and impossible to find our guide. We run to the other side of the station and manage to make out a group of men, marching rapidly into the distance in complete darkness. They are the Poles, and we join up with them. Little by little we get to the head of the group and nearer to our guide. Above all we wanted to find out if anybody had stayed behind at the station. But everything was going as planned, and if you didn't join this marching group using your initiative you could be left behind. Nobody would be bothered. And to think that our guide had specially recommended us!

To start with we follow the main road for 2 kilometres, which is a rather dangerous exercise. A group of thirty marching people could easily provoke a comprehensible curiosity. As soon as we see a car approaching, we all rush into the nearby fields and lie down flat and remain very still. What an incredible start to our trek! Soon we leave the main road going to Foix, and turn left, and take a small minor road that avoids the town.

It's at the beginning of this road that I break my umbrella while leaning a bit too heavily on a pile of stones. All that remains is the handle, which I keep as a souvenir of this lovely brolly which Chiara and I had bought together back in The Hague in 1930. It has given me good service for thirteen years.

Our route continues to climb and we go through dormant villages, along narrow paths and climb onto some hills. We climb a hill known as Le Pech de Foix which is an imposing height of 855 metres. We keep on sliding in the wet grass as the ascent is very steep and challenging. My rucksack is feeling terribly heavy although I already sent back to Chiara many things while in Toulouse. We have to walk very fast as we have to go through the forbidden zone while under cover of night. I lose my spectacles but, thanks to my colleagues, we find them again. Our guide takes my rucksack and carries it for a couple of hours. Then we continue going through some fields. It's a beautiful night without a moon, with clear visibility, and a fantastic starlit sky. Below us we can see the lights of Foix and other villages. We can make out to our right the Ariège mountain peaks, outlined in a sort of melancholy poetry. Our route takes us parallel to the Ariège river.

Day 2: Friday the 1st of October – South of Foix (Ariège)

Our trek continues all night long. At the village of Saint-Paulet we enter into the forbidden zone, and then walk next to the railway line that goes south to Ax-les-Thermes. We go through some woods which are very near some German checkpoints. We can see their lights and have to walk very silently. Talking or smoking is naturally strictly forbidden. Towards the middle of the night, we approach a hazardous point of our journey, which is the bridge over the Ariège river near the village of Marcus. Usually, it is most heavily guarded by a German patrol and floodlit all night. We all lie low in a field about 150 metres away. We await a signal that the patrol has distanced itself for a short while and that the coast is clear. The lantern of a local woman gives us the sign and we immediately run across the bridge as quickly as possible. The bridge shakes and shudders under our heavily hobnailed boots. Finally, we are all safely across the river.

We continue our silent trek through the night and along the banks of the Ariège river. We then avoid the town of Tarascon, going through wet fields with a lot of underground water. We have to cross a little torrent at one point and, as one cannot see the stones lying in its bed, most people stumble into the water, and get wet up to their ankles. Getting wet is terrible news for your feet. If you have water in your mountain boots it causes the leather to get stiff which then injures the skin. Our guides are so brutal and unreasonable and force us to run and we get out of breath. Bobrowski and I decide to stop for a moment to take off our boots to get rid of the water. Our whole group disappears into the distance and we experience a very eerie feeling, but after ten minutes our guide returns and we have an almighty row as he is furious with both of us.

It is now 5 am, and at 5.30 am the workers go to the factory along the main road that we have to cross which is controlled by German patrols. However, we manage to cross it with the help of three guides armed with sub-machine guns. I'm very much impressed by our silent march through the morning mists. Once across the main road we leave the Ariège valley and head in the direction of the higher mountains. When we are across the pass, we shall no longer be visible to the patrols, so we must get there before dawn. The ascent is very steep and everybody is exhausted after this long trek through the sleepless night. We had expected to have a different experience and to be well fed. Anyway, that's what they had promised before we left. But the reality is much harder than we had expected. More disappointments and deceptions will be there, all along our journey.

After the pass, we settle into a clearing in the middle of a fir forest but the earth is very humid and the morning air is relatively fresh. We are near the village of Quié but we have to remain in a prone position all day. My companions are all exhausted and angry.

The officers who were designated to head the expedition lack the necessary authority. But, thanks to the initiative of the group of the escaped prisoners of war, who were by far the most disciplined, we designate Bobrowski as commander of our expedition. I always remained a bit distant but all the same retained proper and cordial relations with everybody. Soon everybody finds out who I was and my companions reveal that I was the Polish government's delegate in France. The choice of Bobrowski turned out to be a very positive one. Although he did not have any officer's rank, he transformed our group, the members of which were an undisciplined lot, into one fired by the spirit of companionship and solidarity. He likes to play the leading part and adores being popular.

Soon we were to witness the result of his first happy initiative.

We decided to buy a whole lamb from a local farmer. It emerged that there were two cooks among our fellow travellers and we all shared the various tasks and everybody got busy. We boil our lamb in a makeshift cauldron and everybody gets a nice chunk of meat. We then clean ourselves up and dry our wet clothes in the sun which has finally come out. We sleep a few hours and time goes by quickly until 7 pm. One of our companions, Captain Serafin, who has heart problems, decides to abandon the trip and goes back with one of the guides.

At 7 pm we set off in the direction of the village of Génat. The view from the pass as we go down into the valley is stunning and one can see in front of us, for the first time, the snowy peaks of the mountains of Andorra. The sunset, with the view towards the valley where we can see peasants with their herds of cows and sheep, and the sound of the cowbells, together with the tranquil atmosphere, is most impressive. I shall always remember this unforgettable spectacle while we were waiting for the coast to be clear to continue our trek. Eventually all the traffic on the road ceases and we then run through the village on tip-toes. This sight of forty-five men running silently in hobnailed boots in the half-light was something unbelievable. It is an excellent school for smugglers!

We are now in the Vicdessos torrent valley and we cross the bridge and the D8 road at Niaux. Here one has to run for some 20 to 30 metres to cross the road. The smugglers' awaited light signal has worked well, and we wait on the rampart, all lying prone until we receive the all-clear to cross the road.

Immediately after crossing the road and the village a German car drives through with blazing lights. We have been most fortunate! Then one of our companions is missing. A moment of general alarm! Our guides find him, but it could have ended badly, for both him and us as well.

We walk to the village of Miglos using the mountain paths. It's here that, with one of my companions, we hire a mule to carry our rucksacks until we get to Andorra. I felt that, without this help, I would be unable to carry on until the end. Also, we are joined here by a group of Spanish smugglers all carrying sacks of lentils. A young man hauls a 42-kilogram motorcycle across the mountains to Andorra! We are a long procession of fifty men and two mules rapidly advancing along the high mountain trails on a moonless, but star-filled night. What a day it has been!

Day 3: Saturday the 2nd of October - Aston valley (France) to El Serrat (Andorra)

The climb becomes more and more difficult. It's very dark in the forests and very tiring as we cannot see where to put our next step. The smugglers go faster with no regard or care for the human cattle that they are leading. At dawn, we find ourselves on the crest of a mountain at a height of about 1900 metres. The view on all sides is fantastic, but it's freezing cold. Below us is the Aston valley which goes right up to the border with Andorra, but we shall avoid all the easy paths for security reasons and we shall have to reach the frontier by the high-altitude trails.

We cross over three parallel mountain crests at a height of about 2000 metres. We rest at the foot of one of these crests and then there is sudden alarm because of a German spotter plane patrolling the frontier. We climb down into the valley of a tributary of the Aston River which separates us from Andorra's mountains and which is fed by some lakes which lie halfway up the mountain. We are constantly feeling very thirsty and tired and swallow the snow that we find in the cracks and crevices.

After crossing several mountain torrents, we eventually get to the bottom of the Port de Baquel pass, at a height of 2546 metres, just before dusk. The scenery is harsh but of an austere beauty. The view to the pass is spectacular. Higher up we find piles of snow and we continually slip as our poor tired legs have been walking, nearly non-stop, for twenty-four hours. They now refuse to go any further! The weaker members declare that they prefer to stay and be captured, rather than continue. They collapse into the snow and our Dr Wierdak administers some drops of valerium and some sugar. Bobrowski shows great energy and courage.

The frontier is now very near as it passes across the top of the pass which gives new strength to the weaker members. Here we are at last at the pass! I'm completely exhausted! Everybody senses the tremendous nervous tension.

My peasant with the mule declares that we have reached Andorra and gives me back my rucksack. Everybody expected him to carry it until we got to the village where we are supposed to spend the night. I accuse our guides that they have tricked us and I call them a bunch of liars. It's a fact that they are repeatedly lying and deceiving us without any qualms. Then our chief guide, young Michel, gets very angry and takes out his gun and threatens me. Two Polish officers grab his hands and we witness a very violent scene right at the top of the pass. Then everybody calms down, thanks to the intervention of Bobrowski and a few others.

We continue our trek and have to descend to the valley

of Valeria del Norte on a snow-covered slope for about one kilometre, in complete darkness, jumping from one stone to another and continuously slipping in the snow. It's real torture, and without the help of a few companions, especially Dr Wierdak and Bobrowski, I don't know if I could have reached the bottom. I was at the end of my strength, and my legs were bent as if they were made of rubber. Our ordeal along the stony trail by the torrent lasts until about 1 am. Many members of our group are in desperation.

Finally, we arrive at the smugglers' village of El Serrat, where we are installed in a barn and sleep in the hay.

Since leaving Saint-Jean-de-Verges we have walked 110 kilometres but mostly on rugged paths and mountain trails and with a combined total climb of 7000 metres. That's not bad for just over two days!

Chapter 3

Andorra

Day 4: Sunday the 3rd of October - El Serrat

The night in the barn was not so bad. It had a certain charm. In the morning I feel a good twenty years younger. We were so tired that we slept well in the hay despite the cold caused by draughts due to the skylights being open. But the high mountain air of 1500 metres acts as a tonic. The sun comes up relatively late in this beautiful valley. From all around comes the noise of mountain streams and waterfalls. How I would love to come back here one day with Chiara.

There reigns that morning a general atmosphere of joy and relaxation. We are so happy that the most challenging moments are behind us. We dry our clothes and our socks and boots. We shave and wash near a drinking trough for animals using a little pocket mirror and by getting into bizarre positions to see our faces. Some of us go for a bit of a stroll but the farmer warns us that we could be observed from above which could cause some complications for both him and us.

For lunch we are divided up into groups of ten or eleven people. A sheep has been specially slaughtered for us. We all get lovely chunks of the meat accompanied by delicious potatoes and nuts. Bobrowski and I have teamed up with a little group, composed of Mr Ogonowski, who is a pharmacist by profession and formerly the chief of our shelter in Uriage; also, Michal, a vet, Wierdak, a doctor, and Hoffmann from Poznan, who was a prisoner of war (POW) in Germany. Each of us comes up with something nice from their own sack to share with the group. I have an excellent lard which Chiara had given me and is much appreciated by everybody. In the afternoon we all get together and people start recounting their war experiences. There are some extraordinary stories. These Poles hail from all over the world and everyone is keen to join up with the national army in England. But it's Hoffmann who has the best stories about the POWs' lives in the concentration camps for prisoners who had tried to escape. My hair stands on end when I hear of the terrible cruelty of the German officers and under-officers.

In the afternoon a worrying rumour starts making the rounds about the Gestapo arresting five Poles in Andorra. Our guide, Michel, went off to Andorra in the morning to see Carlos, the Polish officer who looks after Polish escapes, but he does not come back as planned. Instead, he has sent a messenger with the news of Carlos's failed tentative arrest by Gestapo agents. His deputy was taken prisoner. Carlos has disappeared which means that the Polish office's connection, which was to take care of our onward journey, is now severed. I had been specially recommended to him and I was supposed to have got a car from here. The outlook is bleak and we don't feel very safe any more. Our trip will undoubtedly take more time.

We stay another night in El Serrat. Dinner once again consists of roast lamb and potatoes. In the evening we all get together in the barn and around a brazier we sing military and patriotic songs. In the end we all say our evening prayers together with the good Abbé Krochulac, a young priest who is not too intelligent, but full of verve and goodwill. A typical army chaplain. We hit the hay at about 11 pm. When will we be able to leave this place?

Day 5: Monday the 4th of October – Andorra

We are lucky that the good weather continues. It's the 4th of October which is the wedding anniversary for Chiara and me. A month ago, we had planned to spend this day together in Saint-Chef. Instead, I'm separated from my dear wife by impassable mountains. Soon I shall be even further away!

As soon as I get up, I try to find a quiet spot where I can settle down and read the words that Chiara had prepared for today, which had been written by her on the 28th of September when we parted. Unfortunately, no chance of a Mass or Holy Communion in this wild place.

The day passes quite quickly and we already feel well rested. We are ready to face new challenges but our guide does not return.

Rain forces us to spend the afternoon in the barn. In the evening the guide returns. He did not find Carlos, but the organisation of Spanish smugglers has given us their assurance that they will guide us all the way to Barcelona. What a relief!

We leave at 10 pm. We walk on the road, but the darkness of the night is made worse by light rain. We walk in the direction of Andorra. It's a shame that we can't make this journey by day to enjoy the view of these beautiful mountains whose silhouettes we can dimly make out in the gloom. We march at a brisk and steady pace and after 16 kilometres we stop, just short of the town of Andorra, where we have to await the truck which is supposed to take us further on our journey.

Day 6: Tuesday the 5th of October - Andorra and Spain

At long last our truck arrives and we jump in with our rucksacks. We remain standing, and a big tarpaulin is drawn over everybody which covers us completely. It is strictly forbidden to speak, to smoke, or even to move. We are supposed to be merchandise but we are the merchandise! We are indeed regarded as chattel by our guides and smugglers. They mistreat us without any thought for our physical strength. The journey in the truck lasts about two hours and it's very exhausting as we are all squeezed in, squashed together, and shaken and breathing is difficult.

We disembark on the main road at about 3 am and we notice that we are already at a certain height. Everybody receives some bread and two tins of sardines which, we are told, is all that we shall get today.

We turn left off the road and we immediately start climbing, in nearly complete darkness, in a wild high mountain landscape. However, we console each other with the promise that the route in front of us will not be so exhausting. In fact, our guides are hiding the real truth and are lying so that we don't get too discouraged. If only we had known the great exhaustion that still awaited us!

After a while we realise that we are near the Hospitalet pass, at the spot where the three frontiers of France, Spain and Andorra meet. Initially, our ascent is not very difficult and it starts getting light again. We cross several streams. As dawn breaks, we cross the Col du Portail Blanc in Andorra at a height of about 2600 metres. Next, we follow the Franco-Spanish border along the mountain crests. We see two small lakes below us in a small valley and above us, the grand and majestic mountain peaks.

We take a short rest near a sign which designates the border between Spain and France. Our journey continues on high mountain trails situated near the peak of Pedro de Campcardós at 2900 meters. This part of our trek across the Pyrenees is more complicated than the usual route taken by earlier expeditions. Our guides are wary of descending into the Puigcerdá valley too early because of the latest arrests. We are therefore obliged to take the route that follows the passes and peaks around this valley which prolongs significantly the travel time and imposes an enormous extra strain on our bodies.

Eventually, we catch sight of the Puigcerdá valley and behind it, the Pyrenees' last contours all in a bluish colour in the swirling morning mists. However, the visibility is good. Huge forests adorn the lower reaches of the mountains below us. A little lake appears to be made of silver as it glows in this early morning light. As we descend, we get into the fir forests, but have to take very secondary trails to avoid the constant patrols of the Spanish border guards as this is an area where they are especially active.

These forests possess a certain poetic charm. Huge rocks adorn the clearings and sometimes there are marshes to be avoided and many beautiful brooks and small waterfalls litter the route. We stop for a while within the forest but it's only as dusk approaches that we finally start descending into the Puigcerdá valley. The going is challenging as we have to avoid the usual trails and it is exceedingly tiring especially as we have been walking practically non-stop, for the last twenty-seven hours.

Dominican Convent   Villa de la Tronche in Grenoble

Villa Rose in Villard-de-Lans

Voiron - Chateau de Maubec   Gare de Moirans

St. Jean de Verges railway station

Valley of the Peche de Foix

Tarascon-sur-Ariege

The bridge over the Ariege River

Quie

Genat village sign

A cross in the forest near Genat

Morning mist in Aston valley

Church in Genat

The Aston River

Aston Valley (Lake at the top of the valley)

Niaux - The dangerous road crossing

The Vicdessos River in Niaux

View from Miglos

Approaching the Port de Baquel Pass

Chapter 4

Spain: Puigcerdá to Barcelona

The kind Dr Wierdak is frequently at my side to help me and just giving me his arm as a support is enough. My poor legs feel as if they are made of jelly! My rucksack is being carried by a young man who volunteered to look after it. On the whole everybody is very friendly and respectful towards me and there exists a good team spirit in our group.

As night falls, we continue our descent and perceive the lights of the town of Puigcerdá on our left. It has been a long time since I last saw so many town lights because in France total obscurity exists as a sign of 'passive defence'.

We continue our trek through the fields avoiding the roads and paths and going past several villages in complete silence so as not be noticed by anyone along the way. We have learnt the tricks of smugglers but ours is a long procession as we are nearly fifty people along with the guides, and forty-three of us are Polish. At long last, at about 10 pm, we settle down near a road where the truck to take us to Barcelona should, in theory, be arriving.

We wait in vain for three hours. We are all lying down in a wet and cold field after a walk of twenty-seven hours and without any warm food!

Day 7: Wednesday the 6th of October

It's only at about 1 am that our guides are resigned to the fact that we shall have to find a shelter for the day, as the truck will most likely only come tomorrow. We shall have to spend the day in the forest. They make us walk yet another two hours. We are all nervous and thirsty and we quarrel with our guides who tell us the most unlikely tales.

Finally, at about 3 am, we settle down on the humid ground below the fir trees. We are entirely and utterly frozen stiff. It's practically impossible to sleep under these conditions.

By 6 am everybody is awake and we light a fire. We are starving and we have hardly any bread or food left. All our stocks are exhausted, including tea and coffee. Mr Ogonowski liquefies a bar of chocolate in some boiling water and we feast ourselves with this brew. Our guides promise to bring us something to eat towards evening as they don't dare to make themselves seen during daylight. Little by little the sun rises and the forest is flooded by the sunlight, and becomes an enchanting setting. We fill our lungs with the fragrant air of the forest and we walk barefoot in the grass wet from the morning dew so as to wash them as they are mostly in a catastrophic state. We lie down under the trees and finally we are able to rest well. We pick some of the mushrooms which abound in this area. Our little group prepares an improvised lunch, based on boiled *maslaki* mushrooms and with the last tin of sardines, but hardly any bread.

The day passes quite quickly. At 10 pm, the twenty-nine of us who are in the first group, descend into the valley and walk towards the meeting place. It's here that, in total darkness, we eat the supper provided by our guides. How complicated it is to open a sardine tin in complete darkness!

Towards midnight our truck finally arrives. Seated next to the driver is one of the smugglers wearing the uniform of the Spanish police. It is our safeguard in case of any possible police checks on our route. We either stand, or lie down, in the truck but we are so squeezed together that it's practically impossible to move or to change our position and just breathing is difficult. It is a never-ending torture! There is an ugly scene when one of our group gets hysterical. Our nightmare journey lasts until 7 am when we finally arrive in Barcelona.

Chapter 5

Barcelona

Thursday the 7th of October

Finally, we arrive safe and sound in the suburbs of Barcelona. We have to jump off the lorry very quickly and hide in an enclosed space near a big square. We wait for about half an hour and then several taxis arrive to ferry us, in groups of four or five, to the British Consulate.

We drive through Barcelona's streets, along wide and clean boulevards lined by modern houses and luxurious shops. The sky is blue and the southern sun makes you feel like you could be somewhere in Provence. The vegetation is very tropical and palm trees, olive trees and oleanders are everywhere.

We arrive at the Consulate before it opens but we are accommodated in a waiting room until 9 am. Eventually an employee, a tall blonde English lady, greets us and distributes some cigarettes. As a first step they ask us to fill in a form whereby we declare not to reveal the Consulate's services to anybody. At the same time, we have to sign that we commit ourselves to become part of the Polish Army.

Soon afterwards Father Kopiec, who is the local representative of our organisation, arrives. He does not look particularly resourceful but he immediately gives his full attention to Bobrowski and me. Later he introduces us to a half-crippled

Spaniard who, with trembling hands, takes us by taxi to lodge with a Catalan family, Mr and Mrs Florencio Puigvert, living at 1 Calle Portola in Barcelona's suburb.

It's the lady of the house who comes to greet us. She is a typical Catalan, tall and dark, rather pretty and dressed in a white house dress with red flowers. Our room is spotless. The apartment is very modern and large and most comfortable and commands a lovely view of the surrounding hills. Also, there is a pretty little patio with some trees and cactus plants, very typical of southern Europe.

There are three of us in total staying here as we are joined later by Mr Hoffmann, ex-prisoner of war. He is most talkative but quite pleasant despite his lack of a particular culture. Now we can appreciate and enjoy the comfort of this house which is bathed in Mediterranean sun!

My goodness how exhausted we all feel. In the last stage of our trek, we have covered 50 kilometres on foot, 190 kilometres in the back of a truck, and 3000 metres of mountain climbing. In total, since the start in Saint-Jean-de-Verges in France, we have walked 160 kilometres and climbed a total combined height of over 8000 metres.

Our gracious Catalan lady gives us some condensed milk, which is thinned down in hot water, and some little cakes made with white flour which are both crunchy and delicious! Afterwards we get shaved and washed and jump into bed! We enjoy a deep sleep until about 3 pm, that being the regular hour for lunch in Spain.

We finally meet the master of the house, a somewhat shy and nervous man and looking a bit sickly, but most polite and cultured. He is a full-blooded Catalan and used to enjoy a high-ranking position in the Ministry of Finances during the Revolution and Spanish Civil War. He now has a small photographic workshop in the city centre. Together with a young lady and a young artist, Mrs Puigvert makes up little dolls in Spanish national costumes to sell to tourists along with other souvenirs. The old grandmother does all the cooking. A bit simple-minded, but her cuisine is both excellent and elegant.

Lunch consists of a massive plate of risotto, which is very spicy, followed by meat and fruit. The fruit here is terrific and we feast on bananas, grapes and *boniatos* which is fruit I had never tasted before. It seems that supplies of everyday goods have greatly improved in Spain in the last few months. For us, after the misery in France, this seems to be the land of milk and honey. But I would have willingly given up all these bananas in exchange for my kids and Chiara.

After lunch we go back to bed to enjoy a deep sleep. However, Father Kopiec and a young student from Grenoble come and interrupt our slumber. There is hope that we could continue our journey to Madrid on Monday in a taxi. If we had to wait for the routine transfer it could mean waiting several weeks. There are about 400 Polish soldiers from France waiting for a transfer, some of whom had been here since August.

Dinner is served at 10 pm. It's tough to get used to these extravagant meal times in Spain. It's so unhealthy to go to bed so soon after eating. Spanish people go to bed much later, and entertain friends until late into the night.

Friday the 8th of October

A quiet day of rest. We spend most of the time either in bed or on the patio. It's a splendid day. Over lunch we enjoy a pleasant conversation with the master of the house who speaks passable French. However, his wife and the mother only understand Catalan and Spanish. We make a fuss over their seven-month-old baby who already seems to be most alert. It reminds me of my own home. I show them photos of my children. It's very nostalgic for me.

I spend the day in my pyjamas as they are washing all my underwear. My socks are full of holes after my long trek. I'm waiting for our organisation to lend me some money to buy some socks and shoes. I only have heavy mountain shoes which I can't possibly use in town as it would be too conspicuous. In any case, we are advised not to go out as the police might stop us seeing that we don't possess the proper ID papers. We shall have to wait until we get to Madrid before obtaining the appropriate documents. All other Poles are registered here by the Polish Red Cross as refugees and receive Spanish documents.

Saturday the 9th of October

I wake up in the morning with a bad cold. I continue to go around in my pyjamas, and I feel a bit cold in my room. Around midday, Father Kopiec comes and gives some money to our hostess so that she can buy some shoes and socks for us. Later on, some Poles come to the house to take advantage of a piano to practise some songs. They are rehearsing for a concert planned by the Polish Red Cross.

The weather continues to be very agreeable and we spend a few hours on the lovely patio. Lunch is, as usual, most enjoyable. The *risotto alla catalana* is especially appreciated by all of us.

Father Kopiec comes again to confirm that he has telephoned Madrid to arrange for our car. We shall most likely leave on

Monday evening or Tuesday morning. We already feel well rested and eager to continue our journey, especially to reach England as soon as possible. I have to deliver my report to the government on France's present situation and ask that they send me some money with the utmost urgency.

In the evening I get my new shoes which are yellow, but it's cheap rubbish which will have to do for a few months. At least now I shall be able to go out, but obviously always with much vigilance.

Sunday the 10th of October

A day without sunshine. It doesn't feel like a Sunday. Our hosts are non-believers and don't go to hear Mass. We also don't dare to venture outside given the local restrictions especially for people like us who do not possess the necessary papers.

Mr Kozbanski from Grenoble comes to see me before lunch. He has been in Barcelona since the 22nd of September and helps out at the Red Cross.

We sit down to Sunday lunch at 3 pm like all other days. It's challenging to wait for such a long time, but the food is delicious. Also present is the young Szewczyk, who used to live here and is much loved by our hosts. We feast on grilled blood sausage with mushrooms and fried potatoes. Catalan cooking is rather greasy but the wine is most palatable despite being ordinary house wine. It is very spicy and has a slight taste of sherry. We don't finish our lunch until after 4.30 pm when we retire to our room and sleep until we surface again at 10 pm in time for dinner. What a bore these late meals are! At this hour, we don't feel terribly hungry.

Monday the 11th of October

A warm wind has been blowing all night and it has also rained. The morning is pleasant and clear, but the atmosphere remains somewhat heavy.

With our host we go out to the hairdresser's, which is in the Avenida de la Republica Argentina, to have our hair cut as we looked like savages!

This morning our room-mate, Mr Hoffman, leaves us as he is transferring to the Polish Red Cross. We are rather happy that he has gone as he was something of a bore in the long run. It's not easy living with a semi-intellectual. On the other hand, we get on very well with Bobrowski and always have plenty of subjects to discuss and make the most of our life together. We share everything, and for the moment he saves me as he has a bit of money, which he puts into our shared purse.

After the visit to the hairdresser, we go to a milk-bar and order a bowl of *lecce* and some little white rolls. It is delicious but costly, especially if you calculate the French franc price using the current exchange rate which is presently eighteen francs to one peseta. There is an excellent choice of cakes and sweets in the local confectioners but all at sky-high prices, again if you calculate back into francs.

On getting back to our house I feel as if I'm going to get the 'flu as my temperature is 37.3° Celsius and I only have light strength medicine. I'm a bit worried as we shortly have to face a long journey.

As usual lunch is most tasty. It consists of soup with rice and then chicken and mushrooms followed by fruit.

In the afternoon we are visited by the young Grodecki, son

of Mrs Biesikowska. Towards evening Father Kopec informs us that we shall not be able to leave before Wednesday. Thinking that our departure was imminent, we had bought a magnificent bunch of carnations for our hostess. Flowers are splendid here but, like everything else, very expensive. Our relations with our hosts are most cordial. In the evening they give me an excellent hot grog, and I also take an aspirin.

Tuesday the 12th of October

Today is a national holiday in Spain. Above all, it is a religious feast celebrating the *Señora del Pilar* who was a miraculous virgin from Saragossa but it's also a political one celebrating the Spanish race.

Happily, I feel as fit as a fiddle. It's a glorious day full of sunshine and the air is as clear as a bell. How this country could be happy with this nature and sun. I sometimes feel as if I'm somewhere on the French Riviera.

We enjoy staying on the patio until lunchtime. I'm giving another English lesson to Bobrowski which I had already started a few days ago, and I must admit that the pupil is most talented.

In the afternoon Father Kopec and three other persons come to visit us.

We listen to the radio for the latest news. It seems that Portugal has put their naval bases in the Azores at the disposal of the Allied Forces which has caused quite a sensation in Spain. In Italy there have been no changes since the fall of Naples, which took place whilst we were crossing the Pyrenees.

At about 6 pm, we go out for a short walk in the immediate neighbourhood with Bobrowski and notice that this is a lovely area in which to live. We notice several sumptuous villas surrounded by beautiful sub-tropical gardens and towering pine trees with bougainvillea in flower. Huge new high-rise buildings are also in construction and are interesting from an architectural point of view.

Unusually, we dine at 8.30 pm as our hosts want to go to the cinema, which starts locally at 10 pm. Finally, we are happy to be able to have an early night.

Wednesday the 13th of October

We wake up to grey skies. We spend the whole morning waiting so that we might be able to leave for Madrid. Later on, we go out with our host to visit his photographic workshop and have our usual *lecce* with two little rolls and come back home and have another of our lessons.

At about 5 pm, we are visited by a Spanish collaborator and our Father Kopec informing us that they have to postpone our departure yet again. The earliest we shall be able to leave now is the day after tomorrow, or in other words, on Friday. That makes me very angry and I don't mince my words and tell them a few truths; that I'm most dissatisfied that I, the Polish government's delegate, cannot get the proper support to reach London as soon as possible - furthermore, that everything is moving with an inexplicable slowness and a complete lack of energy. I give them a letter addressed to Mr Szumlakowski, the Polish Ambassador in Madrid, to be sent urgently by overnight mail via the British post. Perhaps this might speed things up?

We go out after they have left to calm ourselves after this little unpleasant storm. The atmosphere is somewhat heavy, and a thunderstorm is brewing up.

I send a card to my dearest daughter Terenia, for her coming Feast Day. I wonder when, and if, she will ever receive it?

Later, we hear on the radio, that Bodoglio's Italy has declared war against Germany. It's clear that Bodoglio wants to save his country's situation and this is a personal success that he has managed to obtain the Allies' approval for his act. This action should certainly improve Italy's position within the United Nations. Meanwhile the Russians have started their offensive on Kiev.

Around 6 pm Captain Rodziewicz and Mr Kunkel, husband of my ex-secretary Mrs Simone, pay us a visit. I update him on the life of his wife in France. They tell us about a group of Poles, whom Bobrowski and I had nearly joined, who had been ambushed by a patrol of the Spanish Civil Guard near the frontier. There was an exchange of gunfire and nine people, including Mrs Winowska, were arrested and put into prison in Spain. How lucky we were! I ask Mr Kunkel to send a telegram to Szumlakowski in Madrid.

Towards 7 pm we are again visited by Father Kopec, very much upset after the scene that I had made the day before with his Spanish collaborator. He goes into a lengthy explanation of the situation and stays for nearly two hours. It would seem that their organisation has exhausted all their funds and that his boss, Louis, has gone to Madrid to get some more money as the present situation is catastrophic. The smugglers have not received any money for several weeks and now threaten to kill Louis and Kopec! They owe them 700,000 pesetas! Why on earth do they offer this service if our government is not willing to come up with the necessary funds? All this can end very badly and those who are waiting for weeks to continue their journey are most demoralised.

Bobrowski and I are in despair as the date of our departure remains so uncertain.

Thursday the 14th of October

After yesterday's storm we enjoy a calm day. It's warm and sunny. We go out with our host and do some shopping and stroll through town. Dressed as I am in shorts, I can attract attention as nobody here goes around in this fashion. I overhear two labourers discussing whether I'm '*Ingles o Aleman?*' They opt for '*Ingles*'.

As we don't have any proper papers and could be stopped and questioned by the police, I'm carrying in my hand a copy of the German daily newspaper *Das Reich* as a safety measure. In that way they might take me to be German which gives me a more or less definite immunity seeing that people are afraid of them as they strongly influence the regime.

With Bobrowski we enjoy a few hours on our host's delightful patio. An excellent lunch at 3 pm with delicious country ham.

Between 6 pm and 8 pm we go out for a long stroll towards the Plaza de Catalonia. The shops are bursting with goods and the streets are crawling with masses of people.

Friday the 15th of October

It's the Feast Day of my darling daughter Terenia. How are my dears coping and how I miss them? I can imagine that they will all be talking about me at the Villa Rose. I'm touched to see in the shop windows of confectioners, cakes with the inscription 'TERESA'. It is a frequent name in Spain, obviously, as she is a Spanish saint.

It's a grey day without sun. We go out for a long walk

between 11 am and just after midday. We also get a visit from two pleasant young students from Grenoble. Later on, Captain Rodziewicz and Mr Kunkel arrive who are the bearers of some good news. Is it perhaps my Terenia who is bringing some good luck? He has received a reply from Szumlakowski to yesterday's telegram:

Ruegole tenga a bien entregar mi amigo Tito Komarnicki este telegrama diciendole aje me alegro mucho poder verle pronto en muestra casa muchos saludos Szumlakowski

which translated is:

I beg you kindly to deliver to my friend Tito Komarnicki this telegram saying to you that I am very happy to be able to see you soon in our home. Many greetings Szumlakowski

Now we have to see how they will organise our transport. The best would be a car with a *corps diplomatique* licence plate. We could then sail through without any difficulties. We are happy that we have finally contacted the outside world as the good Father Kopec didn't ever inform the people who mattered of our arrival here. If I had not stirred things up, we might have waited indefinitely. It seems clear that, right from the beginning, he had no idea who we were and he then asked some people from Grenoble whether I was in fact the delegate of the Polish government.

In the evening we go out for a very long talk not knowing that it would be our goodbye to Barcelona. We follow the main roads of Avenida Lesseps, Paseo de Gratia, Plaza de Catalogna. We are astonished at the splendour of the shops and richness of the cafés and hotels. A most prosperous and imposing city. After the misery of French cities after the Armistice here we have been plunged into the life of luxury and pleasures. It comes as a surprise that Barcelona is such a big city. I was here in 1929 at the time of the big 'Expo', which was very beautiful, but I think that the place has grown immensely since then. All traces of devastation during the Civil War have vanished.

We get back from our walk feeling rather tired only to find a pleasant surprise waiting for us. Terenia must be the good fairy!

Mr Louis, head of the evacuation office in Barcelona, and just back from Madrid, together with Father Kopec, are waiting in our room. Everything has been arranged for our departure tomorrow at 6 am by taxi. Louis excuses himself for all the delays and tries to eradicate the negative impression of slowness and lack of Deputy Kopec's energy. They remain with us for a long time and complain that the people in London have no understanding of the needs of their evacuation service in Spain. There are far too many personal intrigues involved. A foretaste of what to expect in London? It also transpires that Szumlakowski has been recalled from his post, and is no longer the ambassador.

They give us our German passes for the journey which are countersigned by the Spanish authorities in Barcelona. I'm very impressed by the forgery of the German general consulate's rubber stamps in Barcelona and the police headquarters. This time my name is: Otto Henschel Birken.

We do not dine until 10.30 pm, which is a farewell meal and is both generous and tasty. We take our leave of our delightful Catalan family where we have spent nine quiet days of comfort and relaxation.

We are very excited about our forthcoming journey tomorrow. We go to bed at midnight as we don't have many hours for sleep.

Chapter 6

The taxi journey to Madrid

Saturday the 16th of October

Bobrowski and I get up very early at 5 am. Our taxi should arrive at 6 am. I'm shocked that the journey will cost 7500 pesetas, or the equivalent of 130,000 French francs and I calculate what one could buy in France for such a sum. Our driver, a real rough Spaniard, arrives nearly an hour late. We share breakfast with the good Mr Puigvert who also got up early to prepare it specially for us.

We set out at 7 am. The morning air is clear and fresh. We get off to a good start rapidly proceeding through the deserted streets of Barcelona. We are most impressed by the Avenida del Generalissimo Franco, several kilometres long, and lined with palm trees in four rows.

Initially we go through the Catalan countryside which is beautiful but at the same time somewhat sad. The suburbs and villages all seem mostly impoverished. What a contrast with the majestic and opulent Barcelona! The countryside is a bit reminiscent of Italy, but the earth is red here, and so are the flowers. We are full of admiration for the beauty of the Monserrat Mountain range. Our road continues to climb and it's on one of these ascents that we have our first breakdown. It would seem that the reserve petrol jerrycan, which is fixed to the roof of the car, has started to leak. We lose nearly an hour and once we are on our way again, we stop to buy 3 kilos of bananas on which we feast.

After the town of Lerida, we come into a parched land of a high plateau with hardly any vegetation. It's practically a lunar landscape so characteristic of the whole province of Aragon - nothing but mountains scorched by the sun, and fields of stones the colour of elephant skin with russet marks. From time to time, green patches signal the presence of some water.

We are enchanted by this austere beauty and by its exotic colours. Here it's no longer Europe, it's Africa! Unfortunately, we cannot enjoy this landscape which is also sometimes depressing with its sadness because we have to interrupt our journey with constant breakdowns of the car. We are most preoccupied to arrive in Madrid before 10 pm, because, after that hour, all road traffic is forbidden until Monday morning. It's a big question about whether we can make it on time. To stop somewhere on our route could be unpleasant and also dangerous because of our false identity papers.

We arrive in Saragossa at about 2.30 pm and admire from afar the outline of this city which unites something western with a strong oriental touch. Our driver takes us to have lunch in a modest café-restaurant in the suburbs.

Soon we are on our way again but alas the breakdowns continue to haunt us. Twice it's the carburettor but then something more serious happens with the electric starter. It's already evening and dark, and we are still about 180 kilometres away from Madrid when we break down again in the middle of nowhere far away from any human habitation. The wind is blowing and it even starts to rain a bit. Our driver does not possess a torch, 'Oh these sloppy Spaniards!' and he has to work in the dark with great difficulty. From time to time, he stops working and starts to rant and rave in his despair. Our situation is not to be envied. To stay here for the night, with forged ID papers and far away from any habitation and, mostly, with very little money, is not an option.

Finally, our saviour arrives! He is the driver of a car that had been following us for some time. He asks if he can help us. His headlights light up our taxi and permit our driver to continue his repairs more efficiently. He leaves us after an hour and soon afterwards our taxi driver, in one final and super effort to start the motor, finally manages to get the electrical ignition to start the engine. We finally set off again but it's already after midnight. Our driver decides to risk it and we continue our journey. About 30 kilometres away from Madrid, we catch up with our saviour who has now also broken down. We must stop to help him, but it's a real nightmare. It's pouring with rain now and very dark. The other driver decides to abandon his car on the road, and we give him a lift to a small town outside of Madrid.

It's nearly 2 am before we get to Madrid. We've had fantastic luck in not having been stopped by the police, nor by the civil guard, on our journey. It could have ended badly, not only for us, but also for the taxi driver. It's also astonishing that the streets of Madrid are so well lit and full of late-night revellers and night owls. Spanish people go to bed late.

Our taxi takes us to a suburb far from the centre, near to the Calle Galileo. It's a house with a printing press on the ground floor, and we are lodged in a modest apartment overlooking the courtyard. The building serves as the meeting place of the leaders of the Spanish Republican Party. We are greeted at the top of the stairs by a man in a dressing-gown who only speaks Spanish, and two women. They give us some coffee, some biscuits and a fortified *gogel-mogel* (an egg and sugar sweet). We finally get to bed at 3 am absolutely exhausted.

Chapter 7

Waiting in Madrid

Mr. Szumlakowski the Polish Envoy in Madrid

Sunday the 17th of October

We get up at 9 am somewhat rested. We learn that a young Spanish woman who acts as a liaison agent with the chief of the Polish evacuation service had already come earlier in the morning to inquire with our hosts whether we had arrived safely. At about 10 am Alexandre arrives. He seems to be an intelligent and resourceful officer, much better than all those chaps who looked after these matters in Barcelona. For two years he has been responsible for looking after things and often risking his life. Gestapo agents have actively hunted him down and some of his collaborators were captured, thanks to the co-operation of the Spanish authorities. About midday Alexandre takes us by taxi to a place in the town centre where Szumlakowski and his car are waiting for us. We get in and drive away quickly to the Polish Mission. Only once we have arrived at the Polish Mission does Szumlakowski hug me very cordially and I introduce him to Bobrowski. We are both invited to lodge now with the ambassador. The Legation at Calle Lagasca 75 is enormous and pretty and boasts beautiful furniture and magnificent paintings including two by Velasquez.

Szumlakowski denies the rumours that the Spanish authorities do not recognise him as a proper diplomat. Many problems exist and some of his collaborators had to leave but he still manages to retain his diplomatic status and especially with all the necessary contacts.

A very comfortable and huge bedroom along with a bathroom is put at our disposal. It would seem that perhaps our life of misery and sacrifices is coming to an end?

Soon afterwards Mrs Szumlakowska greets me most cordially and introduces me to her children who naturally have grown a lot since I last saw them. The older boy is of the same age as my daughter Terenia and gives the impression of being very intelligent. Her daughter looks somewhat frail and of a pale complexion but very proud and having at the same time a certain sadness in her eyes. Soon afterwards we meet Mrs Szumlakowska's niece who was our guest in Bern in March 1940 when she came from Warsaw with the Duc de Parcent. She has just passed her *Baccalauréate* this year and is very intelligent and most pleasant, but not so pretty. The conversation soon comes round to my wife Chiara and our kids. They much admire the photos of my children that I brought with me.

At 2 pm we sit down to a delicious lunch of pre-war Polish cooking.

Around 5 pm Bobrowski and I go out to explore the town. We walk along the magnificent Paseo de Retiro which is full of Sunday strollers. Madrid does not have the air of a metropolis but it is very monumental with wide spaces and substantial modern buildings, often in an exaggerated style. The central post office, for example, is very ornate and is called 'Our Lady of the Post,' which looks like a temple but in no way resembles a post office

At about 7 pm we go back to the Legation. We learn that little Marysia fractured her arm while playing and her parents, thanks to their contacts, managed to get an X-ray done, despite it being a Sunday. It seems that it's a rather complicated fracture and at around 10 pm the poor little girl, who appears to be very pale and nervous, is taken to see their doctor who does what he can to help her.

We dine at about 9 pm. Alexandre also joins us and we chat until 11 pm. The people present are mostly complaining about the Ministry of Foreign Affairs' lack of any understanding of the situation in Madrid. There is also considerable criticism about the personal intrigues in the London office. We finally get to bed just after midnight.

It seems that Szumlakowski had already sent, before our arrival, two telegrams to London with the text that I had transmitted to him while in Barcelona - one to my brother Waclaw so that he could finally learn of my journey from France and the safe arrival in Spain, and the other, a coded message to Mr Romer who is the minister in charge of evacuations.

Monday the 18th of October

It's a grey, cold and wet morning. We go out with Bobrowski. Szumlakowski lends me his mac as I don't have a coat. We spend the morning at the Prado, which is Spain's national museum and hosts one of the world's best and most famous art collections. We first take in the first part of the Flemish school and finish up with Goya. He is an astounding painter who was a master of depicting the Spanish soul with all its nuances of darkness, passion and gore.

We get back before 2 pm, just in time to enjoy an excellent and generous lunch. Szumlakowski has lunch in town and joins us for coffee and then departs by car for San Sebastian.

In the afternoon we visit the modern part of Madrid, which is where the action is. Calle de Alcala, Puerta del Sol and Avenida José Antonio are all full of elegant cinemas, restaurants, cafés, and hotels. We settle down in a café where I have an espresso coffee and finally enjoy a good cigar after several weeks of abstinence. A real treat!

Over a delicious dinner back at the Legation we discover, from Mrs Szumlakowska, what will most likely be our onward journey. According to her we shall not be going to Lisbon, but to a port on the Portuguese coast where a boat will take us to Gibraltar. Here we shall be deployed and most probably put on a ship to England. Finally, we have learnt something a bit more precise about the continuation of our journey.

Szumlakowski is always so vague when you ask him a definite question, as he never wants to commit himself. We are so angry that he is so prudent and Bobrowski has a visible dislike for the man.

The prospect of such a long voyage in front of us before we get to England is undoubtedly nothing to look forward to. On the other hand, I would like to get to Lisbon to reach our Embassy, where several Paris staff members are currently staying and in charge of various matters concerning France. And when will we get to London? Everything is moving so slowly and nothing seems to be prepared to speed up our journey. Szumlakowski does not appear to be up to the task of the evacuation organisation.

Tuesday the 19th of October.

We spend a morning with Mrs Szumlakowska who drives us personally around Madrid. She is such a nervous driver and never stops talking. She first shows us the most impoverished area where all the city garbage ends up. Particularly poignant is the sight of a long line of small garbage vehicles, often driven by women, or even children. A procession of misery! Later we drive past the Ciudad Universitaria which has risen out of the ashes of buildings destroyed during the Civil War. We then continue towards the Porta de Hierro, where we visit the lovely El Retiro park, part of the Prado Palace, much loved by locals for walks and picnics and boating on a large lake. Back in the town centre we admire the incredible monument to Cervantes, with Don Quixote. Finally, we see the Royal Palace.

Over lunch with the Szumlakowski family we also meet Mr Findeisen whom I had met previously in Perpignan and who now works in the Legation. He appears to have some news for us. He informs us that there are doubts about our scheduled departure for Friday and does not know whether we can travel to Lisbon. We shall most likely leave for Gibraltar with a party of two hundred people coming from Barcelona.

In the afternoon, Bobrowski and I spend yet more hours in the Prado Museum much to our delight. What an amazing treasure house!

Wednesday the 20th of October.

Szumlakowski, who is now back from San Sebastian, promises that we shall undoubtedly leave on Friday, despite the difficulties concerning the convoy.

I will get a diplomatic passport and possibly go to Lisbon. Can I really believe him? For Bobrowski it will be somewhat more difficult as he does not have the right to a diplomatic passport. After a lengthy discussion I finally get his promise that he will do all in his power so that Bobrowski can leave with me.

In the evening we are invited by our hosts to the theatre to see a light opera called *La Venta de Los Gatos*. Some great Spanish flamenco dancing in the first act. It's easy listening music, but the plot is rather gloomy. We do not get to bed until after 1 am.

Thursday the 21st of October

We get up late, and before going out for yet another visit to the Prado, I have a long conversation with Bobrowski about whether it's opportune for him to return to France for two weeks after a brief stay in London. It would be necessary to establish a better connection between London and France compared to the existing system. This idea very much appeals to Bobrowski.

In the middle of the afternoon, I have a visit from a certain Mr Kraczkiewicz who is the delegate of Mr Kot, the Minister of Propaganda. We discuss at some length the different ways of liaison between France and the various Polish diplomatic posts.

Afterwards Bobrowski and I enjoy a delightful walk into town and we stop at the best café in town where we enjoy an excellent cup of coffee with milk and cream cakes. We are both in a very positive mood.

In the evening after dinner, we go with the Szumlakowskis to the Cine Avenida where we see an excellent Spanish film called *El Abonderado* which many consider as one of the best Spanish cinematographic productions of all time.

Friday the 22nd of October

We finally learn that our departure for Portugal is Saturday evening.

About 3.30 pm we leave by car with Miss Romcia, niece of Mrs Szumlakowska and Mr Fiedeisen, for a visit to El Escorial, which is about 40 kilometres away. It's very interesting from the point of view of Spanish history. It's an enormous building and is both a monastery and a royal residence at the same time. We visit the vaults with the tombs of past kings, so elegant and delicate. Interesting to see Philippe II's apartments which are of a monastic austerity. What an idea to have the bedroom overlooking the church's altar? In this way the sick king could follow Mass while remaining in bed. We then continue our tour with Charles IV's apartments containing some magnificent antique furniture and a whole series of remarkable Gobelin tapestries, especially those inspired by Goya. The view from the windows onto the gardens and surrounding mountains is rather sad, but spectacular.

In the evening we receive a coded telegram from London instructing the Legation to procure for Bobrowski and me the necessary Portuguese visas. Finally, a sign of life from the Polish Foreign Office in London. I'm surprised that I had no telegram from my brother Wacio but perhaps he thinks I'm already in Lisbon?

Saturday the 23rd October – Departure for Portugal

After a very last visit to the Prado, I have to be back at the Legation at midday to see various people. I see Szumlakowski who tells me that he had just been on the phone to Lisbon. They received a telegram from my brother Wacio, full of recommendations to ease our onward journey.

I receive my new diplomatic passport which is a significant moment after I had to surrender my previous one in May 1940. It already bears the Portuguese visa. At the offices people know me and ask why my wife Chiara is not with me.

I then meet the Reverend Plater who is the head the Polish Red Cross in Spain. I used to know him as a young priest in Rome, in 1930.

Later I have a long conversation with Szumlakowski about his own very precarious position and the fact that he is being recalled from Madrid. He tries to ask me to help him in his endeavours to remain in Madrid for another four months. It would seem that Potocki has already been named as his successor. I don't want to involve myself into all these delicate matters, and it's evident that he is more concerned about his personal welfare than the loyalty to his country.

We take our leave of the family and I must say that the Szumlakowski family has been most hospitable during our week in Madrid. Was it because he wanted my help in his cause?

View from El Serrat towards the pass which he had just crossed

The barn in El Serrat where they stayed for three nights

View from El Serrat towards Andorra town

The bridge over the river that flows down from El Serrat

View of the pass in Andorra

The point at which three borders meet - Hospitalet Pass

Puicgerda - The Campanar

The old road from Puicgerda to Barcelona

The view onto Barcelona where the villa used to stand

Barcelona - Patio near the former villa

Madrid Post Office

A Velazquez exhibition at the Prado

El Escorial

Street sign of where the Polish legation used to stand

Madrid Polish Legation

The lake in the famous El Retiro park which is part of the Prado

Madrid Atocha Station

Chapter 8

The train journey through Spain and Portugal

Szumlakowski drives us to the Atocha Central railway station. Our train should depart at 9 pm. The reserved carriage for the Polish contingent is already full. Also leaving Madrid are several friends and a whole crowd of other acquaintances and several ex-students of the Villard-de-Lans *lycée*; Mr Durviga who used to give Polish lessons to my daughter Terenia, and two colleagues who only last winter came to saw the firewood at our home. They speak with such tenderness about my adorable daughter Terenia and son Julek. The Polish élite has come to the station to bid their farewells. We go with everybody else to the third-class carriage having declined the first-class privilege offered by Szumlakowski. In this carriage we find many of our old friends from Grenoble.

Our train leaves precisely as advertised at 9 pm. Everybody is very excited and happy to finally leave Spain where many of our companions have had to remain for several weeks. I get involved in many interesting and friendly conversations until very late into the night and find it impossible to sleep. However, at some point, I do manage to doze off for a short while. It's freezing on the train and without a coat I feel half frozen.

Sunday the 24th of October - On the train.

Again, I'm travelling on a Sunday. It's the fourth in a row which has made it impossible for me to attend Mass.

At about 8.30 am we arrive at the station at the Spanish border town of Valencia de Alcantara. I'm on the list of Poles who have been granted Spanish exit visas. This time as Jerzy Bruder, which is my third false identity since my departure from Maubec. Bobrowski is Lutek Wrona. Szumlakowski had assured me that Bobrowski and I would be detached from this convoy at the Portuguese frontier together and redirected to Lisbon. However, this information turns out to be wrong. We are travelling under false names which means that we cannot enter Portugal under our real identities. How complicated! Szumlakowski seems to love these long and complicated ways of doing things. The results of his tactics soon come to light. Upon arriving at the Portuguese frontier station of Marvão, which is very pretty and all white as all the houses in Portugal, we are greeted by a Polish officer and Mr Loret, the attaché of the Polish Legation in Lisbon, and Mr Popis, who is the former valet at the Polish Embassy in Rome, but is now porter at our Legation in Lisbon. Loret hands me a letter from Potworowski who is our ambassador in Lisbon. Unfortunately, we cannot travel to Lisbon for the reasons as mentioned earlier. We shall be travelling with the whole group to Gibraltar. This news is most annoying. It seems that there are unforeseen complications at every step of our journey that prolongs the duration of the trip. When, and if ever, shall we reach London?

We are then treated to an excellent coffee with milk and some lovely white rolls and butter at the station. We are now in the land of milk and honey as far as food is concerned. Portugal is a country that is not involved in the war and only profits from it.

At Marvão, we get offloaded from our Spanish train and get onto a Portuguese one which takes us as far as Entroncamento, where we arrive at about 2.30 pm, and then everybody gets off. Here we meet up again with all the people who had met us at the frontier and have followed us by car. To travel by car is very hazardous and complicated in Portugal due to military manoeuvres. We notice several soldiers at the station and along our route but they don't look very fierce. In contrast, the Spanish soldier looks much more bellicose.

We eat a rather mediocre lunch at Entroncamento with Loret and a Polish officer.

At 5 pm we take our leave and get onto our train. From Marvão we have been upgraded to first class. The Legation in Lisbon arranged this treat for both Bobrowski and me, whereas the rest of our fellow travellers have to remain in third class. The difference in comfort is very evident and we enjoy a good night's sleep in this very luxurious first-class compartment. After all, it's our second night on the train.

During our journey we have to change twice, but the good Mr Popis, who is a real gem of a man, takes good care of us with great zeal. He always tells us in good time when we have to change and also carries our bags. For dinner, he distributes to everybody in our party giant tins of ham, enormous moulds of a magnificent cheese, lovely white rolls and tins of sardines. Impossible to eat all that! We stuff ourselves with these delicacies, and many a joke is made about the rationing and hardships that was endured in France.

It is cold during the night, but we still managed to sleep better than the previous night.

Monday the 25th of October – Travel through Portugal.

We continue our train journey through Portugal which turns out to be a pleasant experience. The vegetation is much greener and varied than in northern Spain. Soon we enter into a more mountainous area and cross several hilly chains before finally arriving onto an immense plain that stretches down to the Atlantic Ocean. The landscape reminds me of the Riviera. I feel as if I've been transplanted to somewhere near the Esterel coast where the rocks are the same deep red and the vegetation is mostly palm and eucalyptus trees. Cork oaks are everywhere and the houses are so white and look happy. It seems that the whole country is having fun!

At about noon we finally arrive at our port of embarkation which is Vila Real de Santo António. At the railway station Mr Brazynski greets us. He was the former attaché at our Ministry, but is now in the army and is responsible for the evacuation services. We are joined by a group of ten people led by Commander Lucki, coming from Lisbon, who will also embark with us for our passage to Gibraltar. The poor fellow had to spend ten days in a Lisbon prison.

We are taken to the Pension Felix, where a room has been reserved for Bobrowski and me.

At 2 pm we are treated to a more than abundant lunch and at 5 pm we board the *Alerte*, a small English boat. I'm introduced to the captain who is a real old salt. He kindly invites me down to his cabin.

At the moment when we finally set sail our group starts

singing *Jeszcze Polska nie zginela* which is the Polish national anthem and means 'Poland is not yet destroyed'. It's a very emotional moment. Farewell Portugal! The crowded port and the coast slowly disappear into the distance. Eventually we are out into an exceptionally calm ocean, which is not always the case, and the captain tells us that, as we are in the equinox season, the weather can quickly change.

We are escorted by a small British warship which remains with us the whole night, as far as Gibraltar. We are not entirely out of the danger zone. There is always the possibility of an attack by a German submarine.

We stay mostly out on deck as it's not so cold and there is little wind. For dinner, the captain invites me to join him and his first mate in his cabin. We talk about the war, and my host reckons that it must surely finish soon and believes that a lot rests with the Soviet army. Not very encouraging for the future!

I go to bed late but hardly undress and keep a life jacket near my bunk. Most of our group sleep on deck where it's easier to breathe than in the cabin where it is stifling hot.

Chapter 9

Gibraltar

Tuesday the 26th of October - Gibraltar

I didn't manage to sleep very much due to the heat and a certain sense of apprehension. I get up at about 6.30 am and have a very cursory wash and then go up on deck. It appears that most people are up already. We seem to be very near to the Rock of Gibraltar. We managed to sail at a fair rate of knots during the night thanks to the calm sea. The sea view of Gibraltar from far away is most impressive. Powerful searchlights installed into the rocks throw shafts of light onto the sea. As we approach, we can see the outlines of impressive warships anchored in the bay which come ever closer to us. Here indeed is the Fortress of the British Lion, and one can sense the calm might of British power.

Count Louis Lubienski, cousin of Micio Lubienski, dressed in a Polish Lieutenant's uniform, greets us at the jetty. He is the first person in a Polish uniform that we have seen since the Armistice in France. I get a cordial welcome from Count Lubienski, who had already been alerted of our imminent arrival. However, he warns us that we might well have to wait a longer time in Gibraltar before flying to England. There are no regular airline connections from here and one can only leave when the occasion presents itself and then, in any case, military personnel always have the priority.

On his way back from his assignment, India's ex-viceroy has already been waiting for seven days, along with his entourage.

We are also welcomed by a British captain, Commander-in-chief of the Port. After the customs' formalities and our registration, we are driven into town to find rooms for us in a hotel. Unfortunately, all the town centre hotels are fully booked so we go slightly outside to the Rock Hotel, where there is a room with two beds. It's a most beautiful hotel enjoying a superb position with a unique view onto the bay and harbour, and within the grounds of a sub-tropical and luxuriant garden.

We rest for a while, and at 1 pm we have lunch in the restaurant. The food is nothing special. Towards the end of our meal, we are joined by Lieutenant Colonel Bledowski who is the successor of Count Lubienski as the official liaison officer in Gibraltar, together with Count Lubienski.

We then go with them to Count Lubienski's apartment in town where we feast on some good whiskey and smoke some fine cigars. We then take a stroll around town and notice that most people are military and naval personnel and hardly a civilian is to be seen. Many Spaniards come to work in Gibraltar during the day and have to leave the fortress at night. The place is full of military vehicles and there are long queues of lorries and many motorcycles. There is certainly no shortage of petrol here.

We dine in the hotel restaurant at 7.30 pm.

Soon afterwards Bobrowski excuses himself as he does not feel very well as he thinks he might be getting the 'flu. I also decide to retire early. It's very bizarre to be here in Gibraltar, already on British soil. One has to admit that our journey has been exciting. Four weeks have elapsed since my separation from my dearest Chiara and since that time how many new impressions.

Wednesday the 27th of October

Poor Bobrowski has got the 'flu and also has a relatively high temperature and stays in bed. I go out all morning to do some shopping for him to buy some pills, fruit and a packet of handkerchiefs.

I go past the army barracks where our officers and recruits are now living. They have just received their new uniforms and there reigns a great sense of agitation.

I go back to the hotel for lunch and later I'm joined at my table by Breslowski and Lubienski. They give me the news that my departure is for that very evening. What a joy! After lunch we all go up to our room to see Bobrowski and find that Dr Makowalski and Mr Kozbonski are already with him.

We then listen to Count Lubienski's very detailed account of the terrible accident which cost the life of General Sikorski and his companions as he was the only Polish witness of this horrendous tragedy. Very emotional is the story of Mr Gralewski who had only just arrived from Poland and, as a special favour, was asked by Sikorski to join him on his plane. It seems that he had left a diary in the form of letters to his wife which had been found among the wreckage in the sea and the last words which he had written were: 'A new chapter of my life is beginning.'

I go with the two officers to change my money into English currency as Gibraltar pounds are not valid in England. Afterwards Mr Breslowski invites me for tea at the Library.

At 6 pm we all go to the central Place of Arms of Gibraltar

to see a poignant military ceremony called the Ceremony of the Keys. It is a historical re-enactment of the locking of the gates to the old town and the garrison of Gibraltar, and has been performed once a week since the beginning of the 18th century. Today is a unique and rare occasion that the keys get consigned to the navy. It's the detachment of the Somerset Light Infantry Regiment which hands over the keys. The soldiers march at a brisk pace and the music of the brass band is terrific. My Polish friends find this ceremony rather theatrical but one has to respect the British love of traditions. I'm so happy to find myself in an Allied country, amongst troops which face up to our common enemy.

At about 7 pm we go back to the hotel with Colonel Bledowski to pack our belongings which, in my case, is just to fill my old rucksack. We wait in the hall for the car to arrive to take us to the airport. It so happens that it's a dance evening at the hotel. We can see military, naval and air force officers dancing away with women who are, either in transit, or members of the Women's Auxilliary Forces. It's something new for me to see women in army uniforms. They seem to be thoroughly enjoying their new military privileges and don't seem to be in any way intimidated by the men.

In the hall I also notice Mr Prunas, the Italian Ambassador in Lisbon, just passing through Gibraltar on his way to Bari in order to visit the King of Italy. We greet each other most cordially as we knew each other well when we were both in Geneva. His wife was also a good friend of my wife Chiara as they both went to the Assumption School in Rome. On this occasion she had decided to remain in Lisbon.

At 9 pm the car finally arrives to take us to the airport which looks very impressive with so many different aircraft of various sizes on the tarmac. Everybody is very polite and tells us that we shall have to wait a while. Amongst the passengers in the waiting room, I notice a very energetic-looking French lady, most elegant and wearing a lovely black velvet beret on which is pinned the golden Cross of Lorraine.

After half an hour we are informed that passengers not having a Portuguese visa will not leave tonight as the plane will be making a stopover in Lisbon. It's also uncertain whether that flight will be able to continue to London.

We go back to the hotel and have a nightcap. In the hotel hall the dancers are still in full swing but the evening soon has to end because of the imposed curfew at 11 pm. We all stand up for *God save the King*.

Thursday the 28th of October – Gibraltar

Bobrowski is feeling a bit better but not yet fully recovered. I settle down to read in the garden of the Rock Hotel. It's a beautiful day and the sun is radiant. The sky and sea are a lovely blue colour, and all round one can enjoy the scent of the tropical vegetation.

At 10.30 am I go downtown to the Polish Military Mission and then, together with Colonel Breslowski and Lubienski, we continue to the British Office situated at The Convent, in order to get my exit permission.

We get a fantastic recommendation from the British Commander of the Fortress for our entry into England. One must admit that Lubienski has been very clever to cultivate the right sort of contacts and enjoys an excellent reputation with the local authorities. To think that he was so severely persecuted by Mr Kot for having been, for the last few months before the war, the private secretary of Beck, who had been the Polish foreign secretary at the outbreak of WWII.

After lunch at the hotel, we go out for a short walk with Bobrowski. Later on, I settle down in the hall to read Neville Henderson's book, *The Failure of the mission*. He was the last British ambassador in Berlin before the war.

Late afternoon we go into town again with Bobrowski, to pay a visit to the barracks to see our brave soldiers. We meet up with the pleasant young man named Grodecki who shows us what they've received in the way of equipment from the British military authorities. The coats, the jumpers, and the shirts all look so smart.

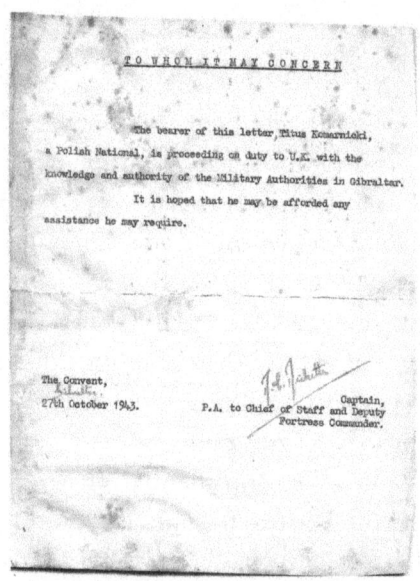

Laissez-passez

Locomotive used in Portugal during the war

Entrochamento Railway station

Valencia de Alcantara railway station (Spanish station on frontier with Portugal)

Marvao railway station on frontier between Spain and Portugal

The red rocks of the Algarve coast

Cork tree

Railway station at Villa Real di San Antonio

Quay at Villa Real di San Antonio

Gibraltar from far away

The flag of Gibraltar

The Rock Hotel Gibraltar

View from the Rock Hotel in Gibraltar

The Convent

Gibraltar view onto harbour from hotel

Gibraltar Airport

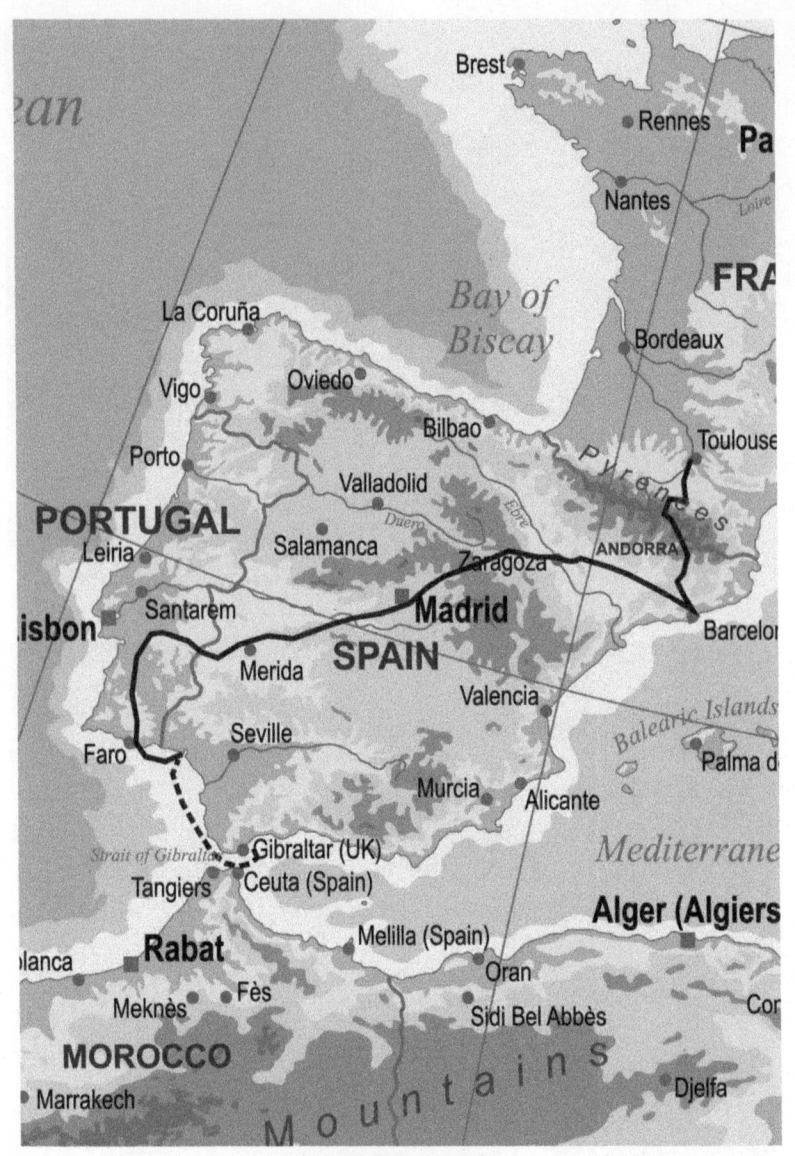

Map of the journey

Chapter 10

The flight to England and arrival

At 10 pm we leave again for the airport accompanied by Colonel Breslowski who stays with us until nearly the last moment. The image of the airport at night is unusual. From time to time, powerful searchlights installed in the rocks sweep the area with a powerful greenish light resembling a full moon. It's like something out of a fantasy film and one loses all sense of reality. And then the airport is plunged again into complete darkness. We await the moment of our departure with some trepidation. It's from here that, last July, General Sikorski left for his fated final journey.

Friday the 29th of October - The flight

Soon after midnight we get to board our plane. We walk towards the aircraft in almost total darkness. One can hear the deafening roar of powerful engines. Finally, we have arrived. It seems to be a massive aircraft with two engines and each wing at least 11 metres long. Our party consists of about twenty passengers, mostly military personnel, an English lady and a Frenchman called '*Lune*' who looks rather Jewish and, I believe, is a courier for General de Gaulle.

We settle down in very comfortable seats and everybody gets two warm blankets. The doors are locked and the lights turned off as we await our departure in total darkness. The engines' roar is deafening, and soon the aircraft starts to move and shake, and taxies towards the runway. At last, we are on our way! We don't even feel when the plane is airborne as, despite its great weight, it takes off with the greatest of ease. What progress since my flight from Geneva to Prague, back in 1937! The balance of the plane seems just perfect and one gets the impression of being on a ship which is sailing along with the utmost serenity. I find it impossible to sleep, firstly because I'm somewhat restless as it's only the second time in my life that I'm flying, and secondly there is the thunderous noise of the engines.

With great emotion I also think that, in a few hours, I shall finally see my brother Wacław whom I've not seen for over four years. The time passes relatively quickly. From time to time, we can get up and help ourselves to sandwiches and hot coffee from thermos flasks, all left at our disposal by the airline. We remain in the dark nearly all night, and it's only occasionally that we can switch on a small overhead light.

Around 7 am the light of dawn starts to filter through the cloth-covered windows. We remove these cloths and see that we are flying among the clouds and manage to get a glimpse of the sea. Far away we can see some little islands and then a peninsula comes into view. It's only later that we learn that this was Land's End, which is the extreme south-west point of England. We fly over fields enveloped in a rapidly thickening mist. We think that we are flying over Ireland, but soon the plane makes a sharp turn and starts to descend for the landing approach.

We land at 8 am in a small airfield. We learn that, because of the thick blanket of fog over England, our pilot received orders to come down in this airfield of Chivenor near Barnstaple, instead of landing in Bristol, which should have been our port of entry.

We settle down in a small pavilion where we shall have to exercise the utmost patience. After a rather cursory medical test in which they examine, most especially, the glands below our ears, we wait for nearly five hours until almost 1 pm. We don't get any tea or breakfast which is most exhausting especially after a whole night spent on a plane. We chat with some junior officers of the Intelligence Service who are real gentlemen, both friendly and educated.

Finally, a senior police agent, who is most probably Jewish as he speaks good German and some Russian, arrives having come specially from Bristol to examine our papers and who appears to be somewhat preoccupied with our particular case. He says that he would love to facilitate our final journey but at the same time he has to follow the regulations. He tries to phone London, but is unable to get a connection. He can't decide whether to send us to the Patriotic School in London, where all people arriving from the continent get temporarily detained. Not being able to make a decision, he opts to send us to London under escort.

We complain not to have had anything to eat and at about 2 pm the airline's company staff finally bring us some sandwiches and tea. It's a good thing that I still had my tin of sardines.

After this frugal meal that we shared with one of the intelligence officers, another police agent comes who, to our great surprise, starts a full search of our belongings just as if we were going to jail. He takes away my watch, all my papers, money and even my mini nail file. The same agent then takes us by car, with our luggage, to the local police station. We wait there until about 4 pm and then proceed with our agent, now in civilian dress, to Barnstaple railway station where we catch our train to London.

Bobrowski and I are under no illusion that we are under police arrest despite the agent's kindness and respect towards us. Our journey is rather long as the train goes via Exeter. We dine together with our policeman in the restaurant car. We chat with him as he is rather talkative and finally, we arrive in London at about 11 pm.

I enjoy admiring the English countryside from our carriage window, not without some emotion as I had not seen it for five years. Those long rows of small houses in the towns, elegant country houses, little churches and peaceful fields with grazing sheep are all a joy to behold.

Despite the strange situation in which we find ourselves, I'm most happy to have arrived in England after such a dangerous journey. But when will I be able to see my brother? Will it be possible tomorrow?

Chapter 11

The endless wait in London

Our arrival at Waterloo station in a complete blackout was not what I was expecting as entry into London. A police officer and a car await us as we get off the train. He drives us through the streets of London, plunged in nearly complete obscurity. After twenty minutes we finally arrive outside a building which looks very much like barracks. Probably a police station? In any case, it's not the Patriotic School. Our policeman explains that the school is entirely full up and that we shall be spending the night here for the time being.

He takes his leave and another fellow takes us through a vast dining room decorated with immense portraits of the leaders of the Allied Forces, interspersed with all the relevant flags. He then leads us to a large and empty bedroom. Next door we can see other dormitories. There are various signs in both Polish and French. Later on, we learn that this is the Patriotic School's Annex, situated in the London County Council's Rest Centre in Gordon Road, Peckham SE15.

Saturday the 30th October 1943 - London

Dawn breaks on my first day in London and coincides with my darling daughter's birthday as well. They wake us up at 7 am and it's still dark outside. We do our morning ablutions in wash-basins reserved for officers and then go to the dining room for our breakfast. We find many Poles - probably about fifty - and many are old acquaintances from France, including a Professor from Villard-de-Lans and some college pupils. Breakfast is rather mediocre.

Afterwards we go up to the first floor where we find the officers' reading room. Most of our men have already been here a couple of weeks waiting their turn to be transferred to the Patriotic School. I hope that this will also not be our fate. It's a rather bleak autumn day, and we feel despondent mostly due to the imposed limit of our liberty of free movement.

I'm given the sad news of Professor Handelsman's tragic death who was assassinated by the Germans. The announcement made by his son, appeared in the *Polish Daily* newspaper just two days ago. He was such a good friend of mine and I'm most upset.

At about 11 am, Bobrowski and I see the superintendent in charge of this establishment. He informs us that he has announced our arrival to the intelligence officer who acts as the liaison with the Patriotic School. They will most likely have also reported this matter to the Polish authorities. This news is reassuring, but all is in vain as nothing happens all day and nobody from outside comes to release us.

I'm afraid that we shall have to wait until Monday for any further formalities due to the upcoming weekend. I wonder whether my brother is aware of our arrival as otherwise he would be most anxious having no news since our departure by plane from Gibraltar?

Lunch at 1 pm is rather mediocre but we eat it nevertheless as we are hungry. Afterwards we go to an office to have our luggage checked and then upstairs to have a medical check-up, which is rather superficial, and the doctor writes 'RM' (right man) in the register.

After dinner at 6 pm and coffee at 9 pm I go to bed at 10 pm feeling very depressed. We shall have to wait until Monday for something to happen. The worst is the impossibility of telling anyone that we are locked-up here. That's terrible!

Later that night we are awakened by an air raid warning and we can hear the anti-aircraft gunfire and the sound of exploding bombs. We climb up to the roof but it's so dark that we can't see anything and can only hear the roar of aircraft engines.

Sunday the 31st of October

Another grey day but warmer than yesterday. We get up at 8 am and go down to another tasteless breakfast at 9 am. We get scrambled eggs made from powdered eggs, bread with margarine and a cup of tea with very little sugar.

At 10 am we go down to a small chapel to hear Mass celebrated by an English priest who has a most amusing way of pronouncing Latin.

We spend the best part of the day in the officers' reading room, chatting with the Polish and Belgian officers. At 1 pm we go down to another mediocre, and very greasy, lunch which has probably been made with rather suspect fat. Afterwards I feel somewhat queasy.

At 2.30 pm we go to the chancellery to fill in our personal documents. We learn of our transfer tomorrow to another building as this one is shutting down. Will this be the opportunity to notify the Polish authorities that I've arrived in London?

At 3 pm we have tea with some colleagues in a side-wing of the building. Some English women and girls serve us tea at tuppence a cup and some tasty cakes at the same price.

At 6 pm we have dinner and afterwards I play a bit of billiards. I go to bed at 10 pm, but very soon after that I hear the air-raid sirens and almost immediately the sound of exploding bombs which appear to be very near which makes me realise that we are now in a country at war.

Monday the 1st of November

It's All Saints Day and the weather is grey, foggy, damp and sad!

At 8 am, we attend Holy Mass, at the Poles' request, in the chapel to honour our dear deceased.

At 9.30 am we are all bundled into police vans for transport to our new location. Who would have foreseen that, barely five years previously, I had come here as the Polish delegate of the International Labour Office, and received in audience by the King at Buckingham Palace, and that I would one day have to suffer such a humiliation!

Our new home is in the Battersea Grammar School building situated in south-west London. It seems to be a very modern establishment with immense and tidy halls, pretty dormitories and all very well equipped from all points of view – a significant improvement on the conditions that we had in Gordon Road. The commander is a military officer and not a policeman. The centre is under military surveillance and not, as previously, a prison-like location. Also, the food is much better.

After our arrival we proceed to an immense assembly hall where the welfare officer gives a speech in bad French, welcoming us most cordially to this new venue. After lunch with Bobrowski, we see Assistant Commander Major Glasgow, in order to present our case. He immediately reassures us that both

Barszczewski and I are on tomorrow's list for the transfer to the Patriotic School, together with a young boy called Rzepecki.

It's a much better atmosphere here. The commander wants to make sure that our forced detainment is as pleasant as possible for so many foreigners who desire to fight in Great Britain's ranks. Everybody had experienced the unpleasant surprise of being deprived of their liberty as soon as they touched English soil.

The commander organises some games and competitions and at least it helps distract the youngsters from their present worries. At 5 pm it's tea time and we get tea with a lovely cheese and a red cabbage salad and buttered sandwiches. Afterwards I take a short stroll in the surrounding grounds but it's raining and somewhat foggy and humid. At 8 pm we get our dinner and by 10 pm I'm tucked up in bed.

The Royal Patriotic School

Tuesday the 2nd of November

We enjoy an excellent night's sleep in our new home. We share the dormitory with all the Polish officers, a Belgian and three Swedes all of whom are volunteers and waiting to join the war effort.

I'm the first to get up at about 7.40 am and then have breakfast at 9.30 am. We then say farewell to our colleagues as we are part of a little group of about fifteen nationalities who are being whisked away to the Patriotic School in the usual police vans. There are some Belgians, French and Swedes, and four of us Poles.

After a twenty-minute journey we arrive in a large park surrounding a huge building imitating a medieval castle. Finally, we have arrived at The Royal Victoria Patriotic School, a foundation for orphans of sailors. Several of the inmates are strolling in the park and I notice Mr Labecki, a former teacher at the Polish School in Villard. There are also many Jews here of different nationalities and some even in Polish uniforms.

The rest of the morning we spend in never-ending formalities of checking our luggage and some particular objects are X-rayed to see if something is hidden. We are also photographed. Afterwards we get to see our dormitory where we occupy our beds among Polish officers. There are several such dormitories and in general there are several hundred people here at any one time.

A bit later while strolling in the park we come across Lieutenant Wolski, the Polish liaison officer. We immediately explain our situation and predicament to him and he promises to do everything possible to facilitate our urgent release.

At 1 pm we enjoy a most pleasant and tasty lunch. Afterwards we go to the welfare officer's office where he gives us 10 shillings each as a weekly pay.

Later I settle down in the officers' reading room but they

ask me to come down to the interrogation office. I'm so happy that finally things are beginning to move and I feel full of hope. There is waiting for me a Polish civilian who claims to know me from Warsaw. We once met, before the war, in a lawyer's office. He informs me that I'm here by mistake and he will do everything in his power to release me as quickly as possible. He apologises that he has to interrogate me but proceeds to do this quickly and does not insist on too many details. I have to tell him about my role in France and under what conditions I had to leave the country. Later I learn that my interrogator's name was Kzymer and he had been put there by the Polish military authorities for the Intelligence Office's disposal. He speaks perfect English. During our conversation he receives several phone calls and to my great surprise tells me that I shall be free to go at about 5.30 pm. Mr Jaczymowski, one of Wacio's staff members, will come to collect me in the ministry's car. I can hardly believe my ears. What a great joy!

They speed up all my exit formalities so that I can be ready for the appointed time. A few minutes after 5.30 pm the greyish-green limousine of the Minister of Justice, with its *corps diplomatique* licence, stops in front of the building's main entrance. Bobrowski and I are both very excited. We say goodbye after having shared our lives for five weeks. I will do everything that I can so that he can also be released tomorrow. My colleagues and the Patriotic School staff are amazed that I'm leaving in such an official manner.

I jump into the car with my rucksack and the car races away through the park and towards the property's main entrance. Finally, I can see my dear brother Wacio and his collaborator waiting outside. What an emotional moment! We rush into each other's arms and hug for a long, long moment!

Here finally is my reward for all the hardships and efforts of my journey!

The car takes us to the Cumberland Hotel at Marble Arch, which is located in the heart of London just opposite Hyde Park, where Wacio has lived for the last two years. The hotel is huge with over a thousand rooms which are all ultra-modern and somewhat in the American style. It's fully booked-up but they install another bed in Wacio's room.

We then proceed to the Grill Room situated in the basement where the food is good. We experience an air-raid warning while eating but the Grill Room also acts as a shelter and the alert soon passes.

All the bright lights dazzle me as well as the abundance of everything that I see around me, but Wacio tells me that this is nothing compared to what it was before. The general level of living has gone down dramatically and many essential goods are no longer available. But I'm comparing it with life in France and find a vast difference. One can also eat in restaurants without tickets to one's heart's content.

After dinner we go out for a stroll and I notice the powerful searchlights sweeping the night sky. We soon come back to the hotel as Wacio finds it difficult to walk very far after eating. I don't see him in good shape as he works too much and has a heart problem. In the spring he had been seriously ill and had had to stay a long time in a hospital in Edinburgh.

We talk well into the night. Wacio gives me some alarming news. He recently received a mysterious postcard from Warsaw, signed most likely by Stacia Zalewska, to inform that our mother had suffered a strong angina pectoris attack and that the doctor comes to see her five times a day. Wacio thinks that whoever wrote this card was perhaps wanting to prepare us for the worst? My God, what sorrow, what sorrow!

My brother - Waclav Komarnicki

Wednesday the 3rd of November

Finally, my first day in London as an ordinary and free citizen and the beginning of a new chapter in my life! Hope overcame despair.

THE END

Notes to accompany the text

From chapter 1

The armistice
The armistice between Italy and the Allies marked the capitulation of the Italian regime. It was signed in great secrecy by General Castellano for Italy and General Dwight D. Eisenhower for the Allies on the 3rd of September 1943 at Cassabile, near Syracuse (Sicily).

Grenoble
This city is the capital of the *département* of Isère and the principal city of the French Alps, situated about 150 km south-east of Lyon. It was here that the headquarters of the Polish resistance movement (Monika) and the Polish Red Cross were situated.

Voiron
Voiron is a small town situated some 10 km north-east of Grenoble.

Château de Maubec (near Voiron)
This was the author's secret hiding place for several months during 1943 after narrowly escaping capture earlier in the year by Gestapo agents.

Monika

Monika was the code name given to the overall Polish underground resistance movement in France during WWII. The founder was Alexandre Kowalkowski, ex-consul general of Poland in Lille in 1941. His organisation expressed the wish of the Polish emigration in France to fight against the Nazi regime. The Polish government-in-exile backed it in London and was headed by General Sikorski.

Many splinter groups sprang up, and it became the second most significant resistance movement in occupied France, after the French Resistance.

Polish Foreign Office

Formerly based in France (Paris, then Angers), the Polish government-in-exile moved its office to London, after the fall of France in 1940.

Angers

This French town hosted the Polish government-in-exile offices during a few months in 1940 until it moved to London.

Vichy government

Vichy France is the French State's common name and was headed by Marshal Philippe Pétain during World War II. The government evacuated from Paris and established itself in Vichy in the unoccupied 'free zone' (*zone libre*) in the southern part of metropolitan France, which included French Algeria. It remained responsible for France's civil administration and its colonial empire.

Pétain's government remained in Vichy as France's nominal government, albeit one obliged by circumstances to collaborate with Germany from November 1942 onwards. The government remained in Vichy until late 1944, when it lost its *de facto* authority due to the invasion of France by the Allied Forces. The government was consequently compelled to relocate to Germany, where it continued to exist on paper until the end of hostilities in Europe.

Polish government-in-exile

This was formed in the early part of the war in the aftermath of Poland's invasion in September 1939 and Poland's subsequent occupation by Germany and the Soviet Union, which brought to an end the Second Polish Republic. Despite Poland's occupation by hostile powers, the government-in-exile exerted considerable influence in Poland during World War II through the Polish underground state's structures and the military arm, known as the *Armia Krajow* (Home Army). Under the government-in-exile's authority, Polish military units that had escaped the occupation, fought under their own commanders as part of the Allied Forces in Europe, Africa, and the Middle East.

The government-in-exile was based in France during 1939 and 1940, first in Paris and then in Angers. From 1940, following the fall of France, the government moved to London and remained in the United Kingdom until its dissolution in 1990 at the end of communism in Poland.

Bouton de Rose

This was the code name for Madame (Mrs) Simone who was a French resistance fighter.

Villard-de-Lans

This small Alpine village, located at a height of over 1000 metres above sea level, on a beautiful plateau, is situated about 30 kilometres away from Grenoble.

It was the home of the only Polish *lycée*, outside of Poland, during World War II. It was also the village where Tytus Komarnicki's wife Chiara and their children Terenia and Juliusz lived between 1942 and 1945.

Waclas or Wacio (pronounced Vacwas and Vacio)

This was the elder brother of Tytus. He was a prominent lawyer and MP in the Polish parliament before the war. He managed to escape from a Russian prison and eventually arrived in the UK where he was nominated the Polish government-in-exile's minister of justice in London.

From chapter 2

Salias de Salat (Occitan) - Salies-du-Salat (French)

This is a small town about 80 kilometres south-west of Toulouse where the Polish resistance movement in France had a 'safe location' for briefings for Polish personnel and escaped prisoners of war wanting to attempt the crossing through Andorra and Spain.

Forbidden zones.

These were areas in France which were particularly tightly controlled by German troops. They were specific zones and, generally, one had to avoid them especially when on escape routes towards Andorra and Spain.

Ariège

This French *département* borders Andorra and Spain. It is the journey's French 'leg'. It is a savage and wild place known to be inhabited by bears and wolves. Luckily, neither Tytus on his epic journey nor us, as photographers, saw any signs of either!

From chapter 3

Andorra's position during World War II

During World War II Andorra remained neutral and was an important smuggling route between Spain and France. Technically it was still at war with Germany as it had been since World War I and it would remain at war long after World War II, only declaring peace in 1958 due to it being left out of the Treaty of Versailles in 1918. Nevertheless, Andorra remained politically neutral throughout the war. It became a relatively safe route for escaping allied pilots and political refugees and also became a spy centre for Nazi agents.

El Serrat

This is a tiny mountain village high up in the Pyrenees mountains on the border between France and Andorra. Today it has become a popular skiing resort.

From chapter 5

Spain's position during World War II

Italian and German intervention had aided the Franco government in the recent Spanish Civil War. However, Franco and Hitler did not achieve an agreement about Spanish participation in the new war, despite its non-belligerency. Spain sent volunteers to fight against the Soviet Union in the Blue Division. As the Allies emerged as possible victors, the regime declared neutrality in July 1943. The removal of Spanish troops from the eastern front ended in March 1944. However Spanish authorities usually turned a blind eye to Nazi activities on its territory.

From chapter 9

Portugal's position during World War II

During World War II Portugal was under the control of the dictator, António de Oliveira Salazar. Early in September 1939, Portugal proclaimed neutrality to avoid a military operation on Portuguese territory. Great Britain welcomed this action. Germany's invasion of France brought the Nazis to the south, which increased Hitler's ability to bring pressures on Portugal and Spain. Lisbon became a safe haven to a scattering of Jews and other refugees from all over Europe. As the war progressed, Portugal gave entry visas to people coming through various rescue operations, on the condition that Portugal would only serve as a transit point. More than 100,000 Jews and other refugees were able to flee Nazi-controlled Europe into freedom, via Lisbon.

From chapter 10

General Sikorski

He was prime minister of the Polish government-in-exile from 1941 until his death, in a fatal plane crash off Gibraltar, in May 1943.

Josef Beck

He was Poland's foreign minister between 1934 and 1939.

From chapter 11

The Royal Patriotic School

Based in the London borough of Wandsworth, this was an interrogation centre for mostly civilian aliens arriving from friendly countries during World War II. The premises were in the grounds of a vast hospital originally intended for orphans of naval casualties. Intelligence officers interviewed incoming alien civilians, refugees and allied soldiers to collect military information about the enemy and the places where the individual had come from and identify enemy agents and possible future allied agents.